TAKE ALL TO NEBRASKA

TAKE
ALL TO NEBRASKA

SOPHUS KEITH WINTHER

UNIVERSITY OF NEBRASKA PRESS
LINCOLN AND LONDON

TO THE MEMORY OF
MY BROTHER
RASMUS

First Bison Book printing: Spring 1976
Most recent printing shown by first digit below:
1   2   3   4   5   6   7   8   9   10

The Bison Book edition is reproduced from the first (1936) edition, published by The Macmillan Company.

Library of Congress Cataloging in Publication Data

Winther, Sophus Keith, 1895–
    Take all to Nebraska.

    "A Bison book."
    Reprint of the 1936 ed. published by Macmillan,
New York.
    I. Title.
PZ3.W7365Tak7   [PS3545.I766]   813'.5'2   75–11672
ISBN 0–8032–5831–3 pbk.
ISBN 0–8032–0861–8

MANUFACTURED IN THE UNITED STATES OF AMERICA

TAKE ALL TO NEBRASKA

I

Peter Grimsen turned and twisted in his seat and then opened his eyes. "Yes," he said to himself, "there is no difference. It is the same as it was." He turned his head from side to side trying by such movements to get rid of the kink in his neck. "God, how stiff a man's neck can get in one of these trains," he said out loud, as if he expected an answer.

The train rattled along through the darkness. Everywhere in the car people were sprawled in sleep. The floor was strewn with dirty papers that seemed never to be still, but moved as if some vile life were in them from one end of the car to the other stirring up a little cloud of dust. The oil lamp gave a grimy light, enough to illuminate the sleeping faces of the travellers. For a moment it seemed to Peter that everyone in the car had deliberately selected a position that would inflict the greatest amount of torture. Some hung their heads out over the aisle, others were bowed forward with their heads dangling loose and unsupported. Still others who were fortunate enough to have a seat to themselves were attempting to stretch out on the short cushions. Their heads hung down into the dust and dirt that eddied about the floor.

On the seats that were unoccupied were suit-cases, coats, blankets, and everywhere the food boxes of the travellers. Some of these were open and empty, but still capable of permeating the car with odors of such remnants as had not been entirely consumed. The closed hot car on this winter night had helped to develop these odors until the atmosphere was close and stifling. In one end of the car was a coal stove which the brakeman had kept red hot all through the night. Those who were in the seats nearest the stove were too warm and had shed their coats, while those at the opposite end of the car were cold in spite of their overcoats and blankets.

Peter Grimsen looked over his family. He shook his head again. This time not to ease out a kink in his neck as much as to relieve a kink that seemed to have tightened into a knot in his brain. It was now the end of the third night since he had left Springfield, Massachusetts, with his family, bound for the rich corn fields of Nebraska. As mile after mile passed under the rattling wheels of the train his doubts about the wisdom of this new move had increased. What would he find in Nebraska? Would it be as harsh and unfriendly as Massachusetts had been? Would it not have been better, after all, to go back to Denmark, even if he had been forced to come home empty handed?

Three years before he had left a small but comfortable farm in Denmark to come to America. He had believed like thousands of others that this was the land of opportunity and plenty, that this was the poor man's haven. In Denmark he could never rise above his station as a small farmer and he could never expect his children to be other than day laborers and small farmers. It was said that in America land could be had for the asking. He could get one hundred and sixty acres of land that were without a stone. The promise of large acres of free land was the lodestar that called to the heart of land-hungry peasant farmers of Europe. They left the warm shelter of their simple homes to cross the great Atlantic in search of land, in the hope of gaining independence, in the faith of a greater destiny for themselves and especially for the children. Peter Grimsen had heard this call.

He sold all his goods at public auction, and after he had purchased tickets for the family he still had four thousand kroner. But he was not aware that in America there was no free land for immigrants on the east coast. All he knew was that there was a settlement of Danes near Springfield, Massachusetts, and to Springfield he came. There in the spring, now three years ago, he had been able to rent, on a cash basis, a forty-acre farm. Instead of deep, black loam free from stones which he had pictured to be the nature of American soil, he found shallow soil and more stones than he had ever encountered in Denmark.

After three years of struggle with an unfriendly soil and all the brutalities of a strange and unfriendly land, he had to admit defeat. His little capital that had seemed like a small fortune when he sailed from Denmark had dwindled away. The hard years of the middle nineties had not helped to bring him prosperity. He had failed, and he was ready to admit it, but he knew that it was the fault of causes he could not have foreseen. At least it was not due to a lack of industry. He and his wife, Meta, had worked from dawn till dark. They had kept milk cows and raised hogs, but every effort had only sunk them deeper and deeper into debt.

Now as he sat in the murky light he had time to think of all this again as he had thought of it many times in the last three days. "Yes," he mused bitterly, "I came to America to get land, to have cattle and hogs. Last spring I butchered ten of the finest hogs I have ever seen, and then when I got to Springfield with them, they offered me only five cents a pound. I drove from shop to shop until the noonday sun became so warm, that I was afraid that the meat might spoil. I knew why I couldn't get the regular price, but not until too late. The market price was from ten to twelve cents, but because I was a Dane, and because I had not made my bargain beforehand I was at the mercy of the shopkeepers. I sold those ten hogs dressed for forty-five dollars."

"Should I have gone back to Denmark?" That was always the end of every revery. Should he have returned to Denmark instead of journeying still farther away into the vast stretches of this unfriendly land? He looked at his wife and five children. The children were all asleep, the smallest, a yellow-haired little girl, asleep in her mother's arms. Meta too slept or pretended to sleep. Peter doubted that. He doubted if she had slept these three nights. He knew that every time she said, "Yes, Peter, let us go West to real farm land," her heart cried out for home. In Denmark she had left her mother, her only living relative. It had been like accepting death of one's own will, for Meta knew that she would never again see her mother alive. People who came to America did not return. She knew that. She also knew that the life would be hard. How glad she had been that she did not bring her mother with her. Peter looked at her again. She seemed to sleep but how could she hold Margaret that way if she slept?

Would this darkness never end? Here sat Peter Grimsen with his family on the way to Nebraska. He had three hundred and fifty dollars with which to start out once again to find a home in America. He could not have gone back to Denmark. He knew that. "Can a man live on companionship?" he asked himself with scorn. But how he longed for the friendliness of the old Danish village, the church, the school, the familiar faces on the street, and best of all, everywhere good, clear Danish, not the endless confusion of a language that he had learned only to understand and speak very imperfectly.

He looked at his watch. It was only three o'clock. But the conductor had said that the train was to reach

Weeping Willow by four in the morning. One hour more, and then they would be there. And then what? Again they would be strangers, for they did not know a soul in Weeping Willow. Sophus Neble in *The Danish Pioneer* had written that there was a large Danish settlement at this town and had encouraged new settlers to come there. That was all Peter Grimsen had to guide him.

And then Meta spoke up. "Will we soon be there, Peter?"

"Yes, in an hour or so. Did you sleep?"

"Well, yes, I think I slept a little. Don't you think we had better try to get some of our things together and wake the children?"

"No, let them sleep as long as possible. It will be bad enough when they wake up at this time of the night anyway."

The train rattled on. The windows of the car were covered on the outside with ice. When the brakeman entered snow blew through the opened door. A long, eery whistle occasionally mingled with the rattling of the wheels. A man across the aisle woke up and blew his nose in a red handkerchief, turned his body into a new position and tried to sleep again. The brakeman entered and threw more coal into the stove. The lamps became more smoky and the stench and dirt of the car seemed to increase with each passing mile.

Most of the people seemed to be emigrants. Although the Grimsens had come West by the way of

Chicago to Weeping Willow, they were now arriving from St. Joseph, Missouri. Why, no one knew. Their destination was a short distance west of Omaha, but instead of being sent direct from Chicago to Omaha they had been shipped to St. Joseph. This had added almost a day to their journey, a fact of which they were not aware, for it was their part to accept what the railroad officials gave them, and not to ask questions.

It was almost four o'clock and the children were all awake and dressed when the conductor came through and told them that the train was an hour or more behind time. So the children's coats were taken off again. They all wanted something to eat so Meta gave them bread and butter from the basket that had held their food for the last three days. The bread was very dry, but the children did not seem to mind that so much. David, who was next to the oldest, seemed to get delight from the fact that he could eat the soft part and throw away the crust without being reprimanded by his father. This in itself seemed like a miracle to him. Three days and nights on the train had not dampened their spirit. Now with their hunger appeased they were ready to start playing again.

Meta and Peter sat silently watching the three oldest moving up and down the dirty aisle. Now they had hooked themselves together with long strings. Alfred, the eldest, who was ten, was playing the part of a locomotive whistling at every stop while David and Hans were the passenger cars and had to do the unloading of passengers. In spite of the noise they made, the other people in the car slept on, for the voices of the children made little impression on the pounding rattle of the train.

For three days, now, Meta and Peter had been waiting for the train to reach Weeping Willow. But what would they find there when they arrived? They did not know a soul, and the English they could speak was very labored and imperfect. Before them lay the new land of Nebraska, behind them tugging at their very heart strings lay Denmark, but so far behind that it seemed only to terrify them all the more to even think about it. Yet they could not forget it, not now when they sat here wondering what shelter they would find for their children and themselves.

"Do you think, Peter, that there will be any Dane at the station?"

"Oh, we'll find someone, don't you worry," said Peter. But his mind was filled with the same thoughts, and more that beat in upon him, hammering in his temples with every beat of his heart.

"The children are so dirty. I must find a place where I can give them a bath and make them something to eat. What if there are no Danes here at all?"

"Didn't the *Pioneer* say there was a big settlement here? Why, this won't be like Massachusetts. You'll see, it will be like coming back to Denmark again."

The train began to slow up and the brakeman came to help Peter Grimsen and his family out onto the platform. It was six o'clock on a December morning in the year 1898, and it was dark, snowing and cold. The train moved away and Peter and Meta each carrying a child and three other little children beside them watched the train pull away. It was dark and cold and lonesome. The station agent was busy putting some boxes into the freight office.

"No one here, Peter."

"No, I guess not, but maybe that man will talk to us when he finishes his work. Here he comes now."

"Was anyone to meet you?"

"No, we thought maybe there would be some Danes down here."

"Nope, no one comes down here at this hour. Where do you want to go?"

"Well, we don't know. We thought we could find some Danes to stay with for a time till we can rent a farm."

"There are Danes here all right, that is, a few. You better come into the waiting room, where there is a fire."

He then helped them carry in their boxes and bags. They made a sad-looking pile on the floor. Two large sacks were stuffed with clothes and bulged in every direction, one suit-case was broken open and clothing protruded from its side. Paper sacks and a large box which had held their food for the past three days looked dirty and dilapidated. There were quilts, blankets and extra coats to swell the ungainly appearance of the Grimsen family baggage.

"There's a Dane has a grocery store just up the street about two blocks," said the agent. "Maybe you could get him to help you. Most of the Danes that come here go to him. You go up this street one block and turn to your right. His name is John Hansen." And with that advice he left the Grimsen family and returned to his office.

"See," said Peter to his wife, "I knew we would find somebody who would help us."

"Yes, you go and see him, Peter. Tell him that the children need a place to rest—and—and—well, you go and see him."

Meta arranged the children in a row on the bench, and sat down herself with Margaret, the baby, still in her arms. She was such a good baby. She hadn't even cried, although there had been no milk for her bottle since midnight. "Now sit still, all of you," said Meta, as though she would be stern with the children, and as though they needed to be quieted. They were too awed by the new surroundings even to talk, but it seemed to give meaning and purpose to her situation for Meta to say that.

Outside Peter was struggling against the cold and darkness to find John Hansen's grocery store. "Will they be up yet, I wonder, and if they are not should I just wait or should I knock on the door?" he wondered.

Yes, here was the grocery store, and there the steps leading up to the living quarters above. The steps were on the outside of the building and covered with snow. Thank God, there was a light. Peter Grimsen walked up the steps and knocked on the door. "Am I become a beggar that I must knock on strangers' doors and ask help for my family?" he thought.

The door opened and in the light from the lamp stood a short, fat, little man who wore glasses and was bald. "Good morning," said Peter. "Are you Mr. Hansen, the grocery man?"

"Yes. Do you want something in the store? I can come right down."

"No. You see we just came in, and we don't know anyone here, so we thought maybe you could help us a little."

"Oh, come in, come in." And Mr. Hansen smiled and shook hands. "My wife isn't up yet, but come in. Do you have a family and where did you come from?"

"Yes, my family is at the station, my wife and five children."

"Well, that's fine, that's fine. I don't know what we'll do with you all, but we'll find a place. You see we only have three rooms here, but then we'll find a place. You wait, I'll put the coffee-pot on and call my wife and then we'll go down to the station. Yes, right away. So you came from. . . . No, where did you come from?"

"From Massachusetts," said Peter, as he thought, "Now this is more than any man could hope for," and then aloud, "But won't this be too much trouble? I don't know how we can thank you."

"Oh, never mind that. We are used to this. You should have seen our place when Hans Nielsen and his family came. There were ten of them, and never

have I seen such squalling children. They came here
straight from Denmark."

He rushed into the bedroom and out again with his
coat in his hand. "Now, let us go to the station."

Outside once more the darkness had turned into a
grey dawn. As they walked to the station John Hansen told about the Danes in the community. There
were just fifteen families and they were pretty well
scattered but they all got together on Sundays, that is
occasionally, and they all had good rent farms. He
talked rapidly explaining everything, asking questions,
but seldom waiting for a reply. He was a little man in
a hurry. What he lacked in stature was compensated for
by speed. Peter could hardly keep up with him as he
led the way back to the station.

2

For five days now they had been cramped into Hansen's apartment. In many ways it had seemed like a
godsend to the Grimsens, for here they had met other
Danes. Saturday had brought many of them to town,
and all who came heard from Hansen about the new
family that had come. They were introduced, and of
all of them Peter had asked the same question, "Do
you know of a farm for rent?"

"Oh, yes," had always been the answer, "but no
place you can move to till March first. March first is
moving day here."

"What shall we do?" Peter had asked Hansen one

night. "It seems that we can't get onto a place till March."

"Don't worry, something will show up, and you are welcome to stay here."

This was very kind of him, and was more his opinion than his wife's. She had her own family to consider. Her children slept on the floor every night with the Grimsen boys in order that Mr. and Mrs. Grimsen might have a bed for themselves and the baby. Meta felt sorry for Mrs. Hansen, for she saw that this was an old story to her. Most of the Danish families in this community had begun their residence in these rooms. She urged Peter to redouble his search for a farm.

Peter spent the days on the street and in the various stores enquiring from every farmer he met. There seemed to be no hope. On the tenth day his household goods which had been shipped from Massachusetts by freight arrived. Now it became a problem what to do with them. Not that there was so much. There were six large boxes which contained their bedding and the few small articles of household effects which they had accumulated in Massachusetts. Among their bedding were three large feather ticks they had brought with them from the old country. One box was devoted entirely to things not for the house. There were two sets of good harness, an axe, a hammer, a saw, some shovels, hoes, and other small implements.

Then one day it all happened without a movement on Peter's part. A man came to the store, and enquired for Peter. "Are you the man who wants to rent a farm?"

"Yes, I am the man," said Peter. And with that the negotiations had begun. The man who called was a renter on a farm seven miles southwest of town. His wife had died two months before, just in the midst of corn-shucking time. He had no children and the crop was so poor that year that when the corn was in the crib it looked as though there would not be enough to pay for the rent. Corn was twenty cents a bushel and he paid three dollars an acre rent. The landlord had protested that he would lose by it, but even so he would give the man one hundred dollars cash and take over the corn in the cribs.

"I know," he said to Peter, "that if I could hold the corn till May it would be worth half again what it is now, but what can you do with a landlord? If you will buy my horses, wagon, cultivator, lister, and plow you can have the whole thing and my lease too, which is good for three more years—you can have it all cheap."

"What is in the house in the way of furniture?"

"There is a bed, tables, four chairs, a heater, and a cook stove."

"You want to sell that too?"

"Yes," and he hesitated for a moment, "yes, all of it. We had been married three years—be three years next month. If I can sell I am going out west to Colorado. You can have it all for three hundred dollars."

"Three hundred dollars. No, I'm afraid that is

more than I can pay, but come up-stairs to the kitchen and I can talk to my wife."

While Peter talked to his wife the man sat by the fire. He was haggard and listless, a young man in years but old in appearance. While Peter talked to Meta, he stood by the window looking at the team and wagon in the street below. Meta looked too. "Isn't that bald-faced horse a sweet animal?" said Meta. "I wish you would give him what he asks, poor man, he looks so sad." Her heart was touched by what Peter told her of him. She saw that his overalls needed patching and that his shirt looked as though it hadn't been washed for a month. "We could use the team and wagon even if we didn't take the farm. Did you ask him about the buildings?"

"Yes, he said there was a fairly good barn, and also a chicken house and a hog house."

"Did he say anything about the house we would have to live in?"

"I didn't ask him," said Peter, "but, I guess it's all right. He has lived there for almost three years."

"I wish you would give him what he asks providing you are satisfied with the place. Then you could go out there with him to look at it."

"All right," said Peter, "I'll go out with him."

"Be sure you look at the house. Remember we have a large family," said Meta. She knew only too well that Peter might not be able to tell her a thing about the house if she didn't warn him beforehand.

3

Thus it had been settled. Peter had bought every-thing for two hundred and seventy-five dollars. The man had complained. He said he had worked for three years on that farm and lost his wife there and now when he paid all his debts he would have about three hundred dollars, counting the hundred the landlord paid him, and a set of harness. Peter Grimsen did not buy the harness. In those three years this renter had paid the landlord one thousand four hundred and forty dollars. "I don't want to mislead you," he said, "he is a hard man. My wife had to carry the drinking water a half mile, from the neighbor's place. He said to me, 'If you want a well, dig one.' But you can't dig a well here in this country. They have to be drilled and that costs money. But you will have kids to carry the water. We wanted kids too, but my wife had an acci-dent in the hay-loft when our first was to be born, and then she couldn't have any more. But she is dead now anyway. I am going to put a gravestone on her resting place before I leave here."

There were groceries to buy and a few other things for the house. And then the boxes of household goods were loaded into the lumber wagon. Peter had bought a cow from a man in town, and now Alfred and David brought her over to the store. She was tied to the back of the wagon. The children were wrapped up in some of the bedding which was taken from one of the boxes and a snug place was made for them in the bottom of the wagon box. Meta sat on the spring seat with Peter holding Margaret in her arms. Peter waved proudly to Mr. Hansen and shouted at the horses.

It was a cold, clear January day, and Peter was proud and happy. He said many times to Meta, "This is a fine team, and a good wagon too." He had ten dollars left of the capital he had brought to Weeping Willow, but what did that matter? Didn't he have a farm now and almost a complete outfit? He needn't worry. As for groceries and anything else, he could get that on credit.

The wagon bumped along slowly over the snow-rutted road. It had been almost noon before they started, and now the sun was already getting low. The frost gleamed on the horses' whiskers, and gathered on the mufflers Peter and his wife were wearing. Their feet hanging free from the high spring seat were cold, and even the children were beginning to complain, in spite of the excitement of this trip through the country to their new home. Once Peter had spoken to them. "See to it that you keep the potatoes well covered so they don't freeze."

It was two o'clock when they topped the last hill. "There it is," said Peter, as he pointed to a farmstead at the foot of the hill about a half mile distant and forty rods in from the road.

"Is that really it?" said Meta in a frightened tone.

"Yes. You didn't think it would be a lord's estate did you?"

She hadn't thought that, and Peter knew she hadn't.

He himself was a little shocked when he looked down the hill at the house and barn. "It will be our home, Meta," he said in a softer tone.

She did not answer just then. She had studied with eager eyes every farmstead they had passed on the road. Some of them had chilled her heart, they looked so pathetic. There were no curtains at the windows, no fences round the yards, most of the houses were unpainted. They were all small. They looked like little wizened men who had grown old before their time. That was the way most of them looked, but here and there they had passed a house that seemed to be quite large and strong-looking, and then she had hoped that her house would be like that. She had wanted many times to say to Peter, "Is our house like that?" when they passed one which looked a little more substantial than the rest.

Now she was glad she hadn't said anything. This looked like the poorest place they had yet seen. There was a little grove of winter-naked box-elders to the north of the house, but the house itself stood out free from the trees in the cold snow-reflected light of the afternoon sun. Meta hadn't known an unpainted house could look as black as this one did. It was two stories, that is, there seemed to be rooms fitted under the roof, for there was a window there, but even with an upstairs this house seemed as low as an ordinary one-story house. It was not only low; it was squat with a single-pitched roof that made it look more like a chicken house than a human dwelling place.

As they drove into the yard she saw that it was built low to the ground so that there was but one step from the snow into the house. There was no porch and two windows were stuffed with paper and rags. One upstairs window, the one opening to the south, was covered completely with large dark boards of varied and ragged lengths nailed onto the window casing.

The wagon was now halted by the kitchen door, which forever after was known as the front door. It opened into the farm yard. It gave a direct contact to the hog house and the barn both at a distance of about thirty yards. Meta's forbodings when she saw the outside of the house were fully justified after she had entered the kitchen door. The floor was of rough board and indescribably dirty. The young widower had cared nothing for cleanliness. In his despair he had simply allowed every kind of filth to accumulate. A small yellow female dog greeted them with a glad bark when they stepped into the room. She had been locked inside for two full days which in itself had added to the filth of unemptied garbage, slop, dirty rags, papers, mud and manure tracked in from the outside. The walls were plastered but in many places the bare laths showed through great holes. In one corner stood the cook stove. It was a large six-hole range. It looked old through its dirt and filth but very substantial. There was also a table and chairs.

There was something so appallingly dirty about the whole room that it was fascinating in an evil way. Meta gazed in consternation, and held her baby close to her breast. "You poor, little darling," she said, "there isn't even a place I can lay you down."

"David, you run out to Dad and have him hand you some blankets, and Alfred, you get the broom and begin to sweep. It's a good thing there will be enough for us to do here," she said, as though speaking to the holes in the plastered walls.

The other parts of the house were less filthy but equally cold and uninviting. When David appeared with the blankets, she dragged the table into the parlor, spread the blankets on the table, and laid her baby there. "Now, Hans, you stand here by the table and see to it that your sister doesn't roll off."

David was now sent for cobs which had to be picked up in the hog pen, for there were no fresh cobs, since the corn was still unshelled. The predecessor had kept a few hogs and these had been fed with ear corn, thus the hog pen was strewn with cobs, many of them on the floor in the hog house. They were dry but fully coated with hog manure which was not so bad at first since it was thoroughly frozen, but later in the evening when the room warmed up, it did not take long to discover what made the house smell like a manure pile. "We'll have to keep the cob box outside," said Peter. "As long as they are frozen they are not bad to handle."

When Peter Grimsen had put his horses away, unharnessed and fed them, he joined in the work in the house. The floor had been swept and water had been brought from a hole in the ice of the creek a hundred yards away. This was heating in a boiler. "What's all this water for?" said Peter.

"For the floor," said Meta.

"The floor? Is the floor to be scrubbed before we eat?"

"Yes, it is. I have never eaten in a pig pen, and I don't intend to start now."

Peter sensed a quality in Meta's voice that didn't invite interference. "All right, Meta. Anyway I have to get fresh water so I'll take a couple of pails and walk over to the neighbors for it."

Night came and the lamp had been lit a long time before they were finally ready to eat. They sat down to a table without cloth, but scrubbed till it shone almost white. The floor was scrubbed, the window sills wiped, the rags taken out of the windows where the panes were broken and paper neatly tacked over the openings. The baby lay in one of their packing boxes that was raised off the floor onto another box. Her bottle was filled with fresh, warm milk from their new cow, for Meta no longer nursed her children. On the table were bread, milk, potatoes, and fried salt pork.

Peter looked around the room with an approving glance. "There aren't many people who could have made this place look so good in so short a time, Meta."

"Oh, it was the boys. They just did everything."

"I fixed the windows, Dad," said Hans who was always sure to claim all the credit that was due him.

"Good. That is very well done, but where did you get the tacks to nail on the paper?"

"I pulled them from the window sills outside," said Hans very proudly, "and I have a whole handful that I didn't even need."

"Put them away so you won't lose them," said the father.

After supper Peter brought several armfuls of hay from the barn and laid it in the corner. On this hay the blankets were spread and the four boys were put down there together. "Now, by God, you'll sleep better than you did on Hansen's carpet," said Peter. The little yellow dog whom Alfred had named Bounce, why nobody knew, had been given her supper. She seemed so delighted with the boys that she had followed their every step since they arrived. Now she crept over into the hay by their bed. "Here," said Peter, "you get out; you can sleep in the barn." He opened the door and gently moved her outside. After a few minutes there was a very small apologetic bark at the door. Meta looked at Peter, but he did not say anything. Again Bounce barked. Meta got up, walked to the door, and opened it. Bounce came in very carefully, looked up at Peter, and then as if sure of herself she went back to the spot she had picked for herself in the hay. By her action she seemed to say, "Now, this, at last, is all that I could ever have asked for. This is really a home."

II

THERE WAS work in God's plenty on Peter Grimsen's farm. Behind him lay a long road that in the dark moments of his struggle led him in imagination back to the old country, but before him lay the reality which spoke to him every minute of his day urging him on. Even in his dreams he saw Denmark only at rare intervals; it was always the new land of America with its great difficulties that disturbed his sleep. "Well, there is one good thing about all this," he said to Meta one day; "we couldn't go back even if we wanted to."

To that she agreed with firm words. Her labors were endless, but she lived in the hope of the future. Each day seemed to promise better things. She had made her house more attractive. Over the gaping holes in the plaster she had pasted newspapers. How pleased she had been the first night after they had dried. They looked so clean and nice. They were copies of *The Danish Pioneer*, and Alfred who could read the Danish stood by the wall reading to the other boys. That first attempt had proved a failure. Before the first morning great holes were eaten in the paper by the mice and rats that infested the house. The paste had been made of flour, and after it hardened it had served as a rare banquet for the rats and mice.

Meta's only comment had been, "Now we know

enough not to do that again." She put a mixture of lye and mustard into hot water and washed all the paper off. She, then with the help of Hans, tacked pieces of flour sacks over the openings. The next time Peter went to town he brought home twenty-five cents worth of unslacked lime. From this whitewash was made and applied to the whole room. "It looks as white as a palace," said Peter, and Meta was proud.

Alfred and David had cleaned the two rooms upstairs where the four boys now slept. From old boards they had built bed frames into which heavy straw ticks were placed for mattresses. They each had a feather tick over them. They were snug and warm. The only thing that had worried them was the rats. More than once one of the boys had awakened in the night to find a rat running over the bed. That problem had solved itself almost entirely. One night the boys had been awakened by a horrible scratching and squealing. Frank, the youngest, was crying in great terror and even Alfred was afraid to get out of bed to light the lamp. Before they could decide what to do, their mother appeared carrying the lantern. It was then clear what had happened. The boys had forgotten to close the door that led from the kitchen to the stairway. This had proved a fair invitation to Bounce, who had come up to sleep on the bed with the boys. During the night a rat, unaware of the newcomer, had taken her usual trip across the bed, only to be snapped by Bounce. The rat seemed almost as big as the dog, but in the end it lay dead. When Meta arrived, Bounce was sys-

tematically biting the rat from one end to the other.
They could all plainly hear the crunching of the bones.
When Bounce had finished this task she very carefully and politely got into the bed again, for she never
ate rats or mice. In the bed she sat with a certain degree
of confidence, as if she knew she had earned her right
to stay there, but out of sheer good manners she could
not lie down until she was properly invited to do so.
This invitation was not slow in coming, and from then
on as long as Bounce stayed in the bed at night there
were no more rats running over the hands and faces
of the children.

There had been improvements everywhere. In the
parlor there were drapes at the one window. They
were made from a white bed sheet, worn too thin for
further use in bed. Meta had worked a very pretty
cross-stitch panel the full length of each drape. She
had used string saved from the unraveled seams of
flour sacks. She had, then, dyed some of this string red
and some green, eventually blending the colors very
effectively in the design on her drapes.

2

The boys had been a big help to her during the
first month because it was still too cold and frosty to
do any work in the field. But every day as the sun
rose farther and farther to the north, Peter grew more
and more impatient to be in the field. He had made
two trips to town since coming to the farm and each

time he had brought home some important new purchase. The first time it had been a dozen hens, and the second time a brood sow.

"What in the world is that long thing dragging behind your wagon, Peter?" Meta had asked when he drove into the yard. She couldn't see the sow in the wagon box, but she could see the long steel rail.

"That's a stalk-breaking rail," said Peter. And then explained that this piece of steel, thirty-two feet long, was a discarded railroad rail and would be used to break the stalks. But she should see it for herself in the morning.

At three o'clock the next morning Peter was at work, for this particular task of stalk-breaking had to be done before the sun rose to soften the frost. The stalks would not snap off after sunrise. After they were broken they had to be raked into windrows and burned.

This was but the beginning of spring work on the Nebraska farm. This type of farming involved a new technique for Peter, but it did not take him long to learn the various steps in the process of raising corn. The small grain farming he understood from the old country. He was seriously handicapped by a shortage of both tools and horses, but he tried to make up for that by long hours of work. While Meta carried on her program for improving their living quarters, he worked from dawn to dark in the fields.

Much of his land was cut up by ditches that made it necessary to break up large fields into smaller tracts which increased the labor. On some of the hills the soil was mostly clay and very poor, but in the lowlands it was a rich, deep, black loam that seemed to teem with promise of rich crops. Hard as the work was, it offered Peter a hope and a challenge. After all he was his own boss on one hundred and sixty acres of land. It was a half mile from one end of his field to the other. "This is no confined and limited peasant farm as people of my class would have at home," he said to himself. "Why when I write home that I am farming one hundred and sixty acres they will either think that I have suddenly become rich or else that I am lying." One hundred and sixty acres and not a stone on it. Not like the little rocky patch of land he had farmed near Springfield, Massachusetts. Here was scope for a man. The breadth and range of it lulled him to sleep at night and lifted him with courage and ambition from his bed in the morning.

He planned to have one hundred acres in corn, fifteen in oats, and the rest was in pasture and wild prairie hay. Then he would have potatoes and other garden vegetables. Next year there would be no shortage. They would not have to eat their potatoes skin and all when this year was over. He would see to that. And there would be salt pork in their pork barrel too and eggs and milk. "By God, you can say what you like," said Peter, "but on a farm one can always have plenty to eat."

"Yes, let us hope so," said Meta who had the immediate problem of seeing that they had something to eat until this magnificent harvest of Peter's became something more than a dream. She usually got three eggs a day from her chickens and two gallons of milk from the cow, but there were many mouths to feed and no meat or bacon to help make the potatoes very tasteful, for they were boiled in their skins and eaten that way. Peter saw to that. If any one of the boys tried to avoid eating the skins he would receive a good rap over the knuckles if Peter could reach him with his fork. David was the only one who would not follow the usual procedure. He always peeled his potatoes first and then put all the skins in his mouth at one time and ate them, washing the bitter taste away with a drink of water. He then enjoyed the rest of his meal eating well-peeled potatoes while the others envied him.

3

When April came there was a slight lull in the work just before corn planting was to begin. Meta had planned something special for this time but as yet she had not mentioned it to Peter. She had not so far succeeded in having Margaret baptized. In Massachusetts there was no Danish Church within ten miles of the place in which they lived. Because they had been planning on leaving there, and because Meta had secretly hoped at times that they might, possibly, go back to Denmark, she had put off the baptism. Many times in her reveries she had seen the beautiful brick church

of her home village. She saw herself standing there
with her daughter at a carved oak altar where she had
stood with her sons, and by her left side stood her own
mother proudly admiring her granddaughter.

That would never be, so now she must find some
way of having her baptized. In Weeping Willow,
Danish Church was held only once a month. And it so
happened that although the family had stayed almost
a month with the Hansens, they had missed the regular monthly service. A Danish preacher came out from
Omaha to conduct these meetings. Meta had learned
that he would come out to the homes of the people to
baptize children and perform other offices of his profession.

Acting upon this knowledge, she had gotten Mrs.
Hansen to arrange for the minister to come to their
home on the third Saturday in April. He would then
stay over night and go to Weeping Willow in the
morning to conduct the regular services there. Meta
had arranged it in this way, because she knew how impossible it would be to get Peter to drive to town on
Sunday, when the horses needed a rest. On the other
hand she knew that he would be going to town on this
particular Saturday before corn planting to do necessary shopping.

She had meant to explain everything to him in good
time, but the days had been so full of labor, and he
was so tired at night that she did not have the heart to
bring up this subject. It was not only the matter of the
preacher that had to be discussed, that was bad enough

in itself; there were other things not so easy to manage. There were things she needed for the house that would arouse stubborn resistance. She must manage somehow, and now it could be put off no longer, for here came Peter to change into clean overalls and get ready for his trip. She called to Alfred to write the grocery list as she dictated it while helping Peter with his change of clothes.

Alfred seemed to be impatient with the way his mother dictated the items to be purchased. "Mother, can't you give them to me a little faster? Why does it take you so long today?"

She made no reply to this remark. She just continued in her own way, "Better get twenty pounds of sugar, because we'll need more now since it will be a month before Peter goes to town again. Then, I think you better get three pounds of coffee, because you know at this time of the year we have coffee a little oftener than we usually do."

Thus she went on explaining her grocery order as Alfred wrote down the items, and while Peter sat by the stove changing his trousers and his shoes. Alfred was very familiar with these explanations. He had learned long ago that his mother had to argue for everything she bought, even groceries. Peter was always complaining that she used too much sugar or coffee or cheese, but if he did not have his cake for afternoon coffee there would be trouble. Meta was compelled to use great diplomacy in making out her order, if she would avoid a protest from Peter.

Alfred was very familiar with his mother's practice in dealing with this problem, but even then, there was something else wrong today. She talked more than usual. "And get two pounds of mince-meat. It would be nice to have some mince-meat pie for Sunday, and then you better get two pounds of dried prunes."

"Now, can't that soon be enough? You'd think I was made of money the way you order," said Peter, in an irritable tone of voice.

"Yes, that's about all, but you know, Peter, the last time we were down to Hans Nielsen's, I saw their new wash basin. You know it is porcelain and has a porcelain pitcher to go with it. I thought maybe we could get such a set. It only costs one dollar and fifty cents."

"A porcelain wash basin—and a pitcher—now what in the devil's name should we have that for? It surely beats all, the things you can think of. A porcelain wash basin! Now, if that wouldn't make even a saint swear. I can't get over it, a porcelain pitcher, too. Meta, are you in your right senses today, or what is the matter? What in God's name should we have a porcelain wash basin for? Tell me that!"

Meta knew this was coming, and she had rehearsed the scene often in her own mind, formulating her arguments to meet his objections. "It's not just those two articles, for there are three pieces in the set. There is also a porcelain pot with a handle and a cover for the bedroom. Now...."

"A pot! So we must have a porcelain pot! Now who is that for? Have we become so refined that we must begin . . . in porcelain? This is going too far—just too far!"

"Can't you wait till I get through, Peter? Pastor Williamson is to come home from town with you, and he is to stay over night with us, so that Margaret can be baptized tomorrow morning. I arranged it that way so that you would not have to drive into town again tomorrow. We can't offer him an old gallon syrup pail like the boys use up-stairs. You know that. And then if we have the other two pieces, he can wash up there too, and I can hang a clean towel for him, so that it will look a little bit civilized. I can't bear the shame of it as it is. It's almost more than a mortal can endure."

"So it's for the pastor. Well, if he is too good to use a syrup can, let him hold his water. I'm damned if I spend money for such finery. As though I didn't have enough to worry about already, with all the things I need for the farm, including seedcorn, which I must get today. We buy and buy, but we have nothing to sell. How long do you think that can go on?"

Meta let him talk on uninterrupted. She knew that after he had gone over his grievances, he would feel better. While he talked she placed coffee cups on the table and a plate of coffee cake. "Now, Peter, have a cup of coffee." She acted as though she intended to say no more about the porcelain set.

"How is the pastor to get back to town tomorrow? I am sure he is too much of a gentleman to walk," said Peter covering his desire for information with a shade of sarcasm.

"Oh, no, I have arranged for Olson and his wife to take him in. They only have to come a mile out of their way, and they said they would be glad to. They are going to come over here in time for the baptism and then we'll all just have a little coffee. That's why I want the mince-meat so that we can have a pie." Then after a brief pause, she added, "You know, Peter, I don't like to see our daughter baptized in a tin wash basin."

Peter said no more. He drank his coffee in silence and went out to hitch up the horses. While Alfred held them at the door, he came back into the kitchen for some tobacco. As he filled his pipe he said, "Can they be bought on credit?"

"Yes, you get them at Hansen's. There are two different kinds. One is plain white and the other has some blue designs on the sides. They cost twenty-five cents more. The plain white set is good enough."

"Oh, we can just as well have the other set. It will look prettier, I guess."

4

The pastor came home with Peter. He was a kindly, rather fat, old man. He said, "God bless you" to each of the boys as they were presented to him. He tried to be real pleasant, but for the boys this Saturday night was an ordeal. There was a blight over their spirits, a solemn atmosphere in the house, that nothing could disperse. Supper was to be a real occasion, for Peter had brought home some meat in honor of the pastor.

The boys were all sent to the wash basin and thoroughly scrubbed before they came to the table. At last Meta sat down. No sooner had she seated herself than David reached for the potatoes. "David," said his father, "are you so hungry you can't wait for the blessing?" This so startled all the boys that once more the gloom settled over them. With bowed heads they listened while the pastor thanked God for all sorts of things which seemed quite ridiculous to the children. He thanked for the good home, for their prosperity, for their health and happiness. "Will there never be an end to this?" thought Alfred who sat nearest to him. The boys didn't mind having their father offer a blessing. He did it only on great holidays such as Christmas and New Year, and then he was always brief. It seemed as though this praying would go on until the potatoes, all of them peeled tonight, would be as cold as a snowball. Even Bounce seemed to grow impatient, and after sitting up very prettily for a longer time than was usually necessary in order to have either Hans or David slip her some morsel, she gave a little peremptory bark. Perhaps it was this, or else he had really exhausted the full list of the things for which he believed the Grimsen family should be thankful,—at least the prayer ended.

Even Meta laughed with the boys over Bounce's bark in the days to come after this solemn affair. Bounce had saved them again was the way the boys felt about it. She got little precious pieces of meat from the plates of the three oldest boys that night, and she accepted it as though it were her right. She was very heavy with pups these days and arrogated to herself all sorts of privileges that she would not have dreamed of demanding a month earlier. She was the only one in the family who had made an auditory protest to the pastor, which was ironical enough, since she was the only one for whom everything the pastor said was a literal truth. It was as though God had told the pastor about how happy Peter Grimsen's dog was and what a fine home she had, and the pastor being absent-minded and a little careless of what God said to him, had thought God was speaking of the family's good fortune and not the dog's.

The discomforts at the supper table were mild compared with those experienced up-stairs at bed time. Three of the boys slept together in one bed, while David was elected to sleep with the minister. He made them all kneel by the bed and say the Lord's Prayer with him. It was like having some terrible blight fall over their room. Not one word of conversation could they exchange with one another. They missed Bounce, because their mother had carefully explained to them that on this night they would not be permitted to have Bounce in the bedroom. A box with straw and a blanket was fixed for her in the kitchen. Meta was afraid she would protest, but when Bounce saw the pastor go upstairs, she seemed to be resigned to her place in the kitchen.

The pastor was a nice old man in spite of his habits and manners which antagonized and frightened the children. Their parents enjoyed his visit, for he could tell them many things about Danish families in other parts of Eastern Nebraska and Western Iowa. He had seen many of them begin in poorer circumstances than the Grimsen's and they had all gotten ahead. Many of them now owned their own farms, not without a mortgage, it was true, but still they owned them and grew more prosperous from year to year. "If you will only trust in God, you will succeed," said the pastor.

In the morning the Olsons came as they had promised. Meta proudly held her daughter at the white porcelain basin with blue flowers on it while the pastor performed the ceremony. Then there was coffee served with fresh warm mince-meat pies, which Meta had baked that morning while all the others were still in bed. She had made a special little one for David, which was his reward for having to sleep with the pastor. "So. Is this little fellow your favorite son?" said he, patting David on the head.

"Yes, today he is," said Meta.

At ten o'clock it was all over and Meta held in her hand a fine big baptismal certificate with little angels done in colors on the margin and Margaret Meta Grimsen written in ink on the blank space provided for the name. Peter gave the minister a silver dollar, very nearly the last one he had. The minister climbed into the back seat of the Olson's spring wagon and was driven away. All the boys had to stand in a row with their parents to watch the departure.

5

Now a new worry came over the boys. One night Bounce stood at the foot of the stairs and wouldn't come up when both David and Hans called her. "Now if she isn't putting on airs," said Peter.

"You'll have to carry her up, David," said Meta.

For the next week every night Bounce demanded that she be carried up to bed. Peter grumbled a little and said, "Before you know it she'll be having her pups in bed."

"Oh, no, her time is not near enough for that," said Meta. What she really thought was not easy to tell, but she did not seem surprised the next morning when she called the boys, to be answered by the wildest commotion. Such shouting and exclamation that even Peter was wakened and came running in his underwear to see what was the matter.

He started to scold the boys for the way they had frightened him, but Meta said, "No, no, Peter," and then he joined the rest in looking at a fine litter of six pups. Bounce was so proud she couldn't keep her eyes open, but had to close them every once in a while to make herself look unconcerned. The bed was quite wet where she had been, but no one cared about that.

That afternoon Meta saw David carry water upstairs in the new chamber pail. She asked him what that was for, but he didn't answer. Everything was so quiet up there that she went to the head of the stairs and looked up. There she saw Alfred in his father's coat, a stiff collar and tie around his neck, and a book in his hand. David and Hans were each holding a puppy. Alfred read a long list of nonsense syllables from the book and then dipping his finger in the water in the chamber pail, he sprinkled the dog David was holding, saying, "In the name of the Father, the Son, and the Holy Ghost, I baptize you, Hobson," then repeating the dip into the water, he turned to Hans' pup and said, "In the name of the Father, the Son, and the Holy Ghost, I baptize you, Dewey."

The next day their father asked them which two were Hobson and Dewey. He then took the four others and put them in a sack and carried them away. Not a voice was raised in protest, but each one of the boys looked pale with sorrow. Their mother had already explained to them that Peter did not want Bounce to raise more than two puppies. She had tried to make it easy for the boys by telling them that it was all to be done for Bounce's sake, that she could not be well and healthy if she had to feed that many dogs. "But, why did she have so many then if she can't feed them?" said David.

"I don't know," said Meta, "but that is the way it is," and then as if to help her out of the difficult situation she said, "Many are called but few are chosen."

III

THE FIELDS were black with the long listed rows of newly planted corn. Peter Grimsen had been compelled to buy a third horse, for the lister required three horses. He had gotten this horse from Jacob Paulsen, a Dane who lived not far from the Grimsen place. Peter had to buy it on credit, and Paulsen had charged him a hundred and fifty dollars. Everyone told Peter that he had paid fifty dollars more than the horse was worth, and he knew they spoke the truth, but he had to have the horse and he had to buy on credit.

Now the fields were all listed and every day Peter Grimsen could be seen on his hands and knees crawling along the rows scratching the dirt to find the planted seeds. He would dig up at least ten in a row to see if they were sprouting and to see how well the drill had spaced them. Each morning before beginning his work of repairing fences, improving the sheds and barn with old pieces of lumber, he would take a rapid turn into the field to see how the corn was sprouting. Each time he was well pleased. Scarcely ever did he find a seed that did not seem fertile. In the mornings he was proud as he gazed over his wide expanse of land. "Why, it's like a lord's place in the old country," he would say to himself. "This is my farm, and my hundred acres of corn." He always called it a hundred acres for that is what he had planned to have, but by the time one field had been set aside for oats, another for wheat, and with the pasture and waste land along the creeks, he really had only ninety acres in corn. Once, when he was figuring his yield on the basis of a hundred acres, Meta had reminded him that there couldn't be more than ninety, but she had met with such a storm of criticism, that she never brought that subject up again. He would "By God, have a hundred acres of corn." Meta wanted to call him "Big Claus," but she didn't dare. Nor did she care. If he wanted to call ninety a hundred that was all right with her. She had problems enough of her own.

The corn came peeping through the ground, and before Peter could take count of the days, he was in the midst of cultivating the first time. Every day from dawn till dark he labored in the fields. His two oldest sons were with him all day long. Their task was to pull morning-glories that in certain parts of the field threatened to choke the life out of the tender shoots.

These weeds that looked so beautiful with their vari-colored blooms in the morning dew came to be the ugliest and most hated of all plants to the boys. All day long they crawled on their hands and knees under the burning Nebraska sun pulling endless strings of morning-glories. Their hands became brown with the drying sticky juice of the weeds, and then as time went on the skin became wrinkled and drawn until it cracked into open sores. One morning Peter saw David walking away from the morning-glory patch headed in the direction of home.

"What can be the matter now?" thought Peter, and called to his son. When David, who was nine years old came over to his father, Peter saw he was crying. Before Peter could say anything, David spoke through his tears.

"Dad, I won't pull more morning-glories. I can't. Look at my hands."

Peter saw that one of his hands was covered with blood from a deep crack on one finger. When he examined the hands closely he saw that both hands were full of cracks although only one was bleeding. "But, David, we must pull the weeds. If we don't, how are we to have corn? Here, let me tie a piece of my handkerchief around that finger, and then you go back to work. They will feel better after you get them limbered up a bit."

"No, I won't do it," said David. "I am going home."

"What's this you say? You tell your father you won't do something he tells you to? That's a nice way to talk to your father. You'll do what I tell you, and I'll teach you a lesson into the bargain." He unhooked a strap from the handle of his cultivator and whipped David across the back and on his bare legs till great red welts rose on the sun-tanned skin. David screamed for mercy. "Will you go back to work, then?"

"Yes, yes, oh, Dad, stop, stop."

His father released him, and he ran across the field to where Alfred was working, threw himself down in the corn rows to continue his crying. "God damn him," said Alfred. "Here, David, take a chew. It will make you feel better and then if you spit the tobacco juice on the sore hands it won't hurt so much." This worked the charm. Both of the boys chewed tobacco, replenishing their supply from their father's plugs by a system of ingenious slicing.

2

It was a rich summer with rain and sunshine. The corn flourished, the wheat yielded thirty bushels to the acre. Peter Grimsen bought lumber for a granary in which he now stored over five hundred bushels of oats. He had received two heifer calves in payment for rent on his pasture to a neighbor who had more stock than could be kept on his own farm. He had sold his wheat and paid for his extra horse, and he had bought another cow, while his first one, now known by the name of "Old Red," had brought him still another heifer-calf. In the barn yard there were over eighty chickens, the result of Meta's careful management.

There had been fried chicken for the table late in the summer, and new potatoes, and peas, and now the tomatoes were ripening in the garden. Meta had also planted watermelon seeds. Every day the boys would go to the garden to see the wonder of these great round watermelons. Then came a day when the first melon, not quite ripe, was served. What a luxury this was! Meta had served it in great slices, and the boys had

held it in their hands and eaten it to the green
rind. This was on a Saturday noon. The next day
the whole family went to Hans Nielsen's for Sunday
dinner.

How the talk had flown through the air that day.
Talk of the old country, of new Danes that were coming from Denmark, friends and relatives of the Jen-
sen's north of town. Talk of the children and how they
were growing, of the way to can vegetables and fruits.
And among the men, as they walked over Nielsen's
fields, talk of the prospects of yield per acre, of the
price of corn, of how many acres there were in corn on
Nielsen's place, on Grimsen's farm, of their horses,
cows, and pigs, of how well this man's eleven-year-old
son could run a cultivator, and of how that man's son
could manage a team of horses. Then late in the afternoon over coffee and cake, again the talk turned more
slowly and quietly to friends and relatives in Denmark. They told the news of how Rasmusen's mother
had died. They said she died of sorrow because all her
sons left her to come to America, and they spoke of the
"piece in *The Pioneer*" in which Sophus Neble had told
a story of how the old folks at home waited and waited
for letters from their sons and daughters in the new
land, and how they must not forget to write. "Remember," he had written, "that while you work on your
farms here there are the old folks in the little thatched
cottage in the village. Every Sunday on their way to
church they walk through the graveyard where your
ancestors are buried, where you were christened and

confirmed, but never in their comings and their goings do they have more than the memories of you, you the sons and daughters who have travelled to a far-off land. Write to them, send them pictures of your children. Don't forget the old folks." And then some of the women had hurried to the stove to shuffle the coffee-pot and wipe a tear from their eyes with the lifted end of an apron.

The coffee over, a stronger note again predominated as Peter said he must go home to his stock, for when one has so many cattle and horses and chickens he can't waste time in foolish visiting. "No, no, that's right," said everyone, pleasantly overlooking the fact that Peter had only one horse at home besides the two that were now being hitched to his lumber wagon.

When they reached home, Hans ran to the watermelon patch, for his mother had promised them all a slice of melon before beginning the evening chores. Then they heard Hans scream and yell as though some animal had attacked him. The whole family ran to the garden to see what was the matter, for Hans was inarticulate with emotion. There lay their melons smashed open to the sun and full of ants and all sorts of little crawling bugs. While they had been away a group of boys had entered their patch, eaten all they could hold and systematically smashed the rest. "Now, I'll be damned," said Peter. "Here, Hans, you can eat a little of this broken one." But Hans continued to cry, and walked back to the house. Meta said nothing. She turned and followed Hans. The others followed her in silence. Later in the season three small melons, that had been overlooked, ripened. They were very sweet.

3

The soft yellow rays of the September sun fell over Peter Grimsen's fields. Everywhere the corn looked bowed and heavy with fertility. Great long ears as if getting ready for delivery from their parent stock had fallen from the pointed upright position. They now hung down and the rich brown silk, like an old man's beard waved in the gentle September breezes. The air was as soft as goose down. The cattle were quiet and lazy in the pasture, the horses hung their heads as if enjoying the rest after a long season of work. The fall plowing was over and in the world of Nebraska man and nature alike were breathing in an Indian summer peace, a peace that follows a long battle fought to a good end.

For the children in Peter Grimsen's home these peaceful days were almost over. They waited for September the fifteenth with a feeling of intense expectancy, for on that day they would make their first appearance at a Nebraska school. There had been too many things to do in getting settled that first spring for them to get time to go to school. Now it could be put off no longer. They must join the other children of their district at the country school which lay at the opposite corner of the section on which their house stood. It was two miles by the road.

At last the day came. It was eight o'clock in the morning of the fifteenth day of September. Alfred and David were mildly excited. They had attended school in Massachusetts and thought they knew what to expect. It was not so with Hans. This was to be his first day. This was the day he had waited for—even dreamed about. School to him was something so wonderful that he had scarcely dared to talk about it, much less ask any specific questions on the subject. Like the reader who fears to talk about a certain novel he has just begun with someone who had already finished it, because he fears that his friend will reveal the plot to him and thus spoil the pleasure that comes through a slow gradual revelation, so Hans did not want to be told too much about school. He wanted to find out for himself.

Today he would find out all about school in Nebraska. He was so tense with expectation that he could hardly talk. His mother had combed his long yellow curls so that they showed off to the best advantage, and his cream-colored blouse with ruffled collar was perfectly ironed. The other boys also wore freshly ironed shirts, and new overalls, but since Hans was still so small he was a little privileged, and hence the blouse and the short pants, black stockings and newly polished shoes.

Meta had been working over the boys for over an hour preparing their lunch, helping them dress, inspecting their ears to see that they had really washed themselves clean. She wanted everyone at school to be as proud of her children as she was. "You're going to be clean. Do you understand that?" she said as if scolding them. "David, you are always so slow lacing your shoes. If you don't hurry you'll be late."

Hans gripped his red tobacco box in which he was to carry his lunch. "Mother, I won't be late. I'll never be late," and then as if he couldn't resist just one question about school, he said, "Do you think I'll learn to read today?"

"No, Hans, not the first day, but it won't take you long." There was a sad quality in her voice this morning which all the boys noticed, but did not understand. She knew no more about the school to which they were going than they did, but she sensed that everything would not be easy for them. Alfred and David both spoke English, but Hans knew only a few English words which he mixed with the Danish when he played with his brothers. The older ones had gone to school in Massachusetts, and their mother could not forget how they had been treated there on their first day in school. The red shoes Alfred had worn, new ones beautifully made, that she had brought from Denmark, had caused a near riot at school. Although it had been a cold day in March, Alfred had thrown them away and walked home barefooted, because the other children had made so much fun of them.

She hoped that everything would be different here. At least the older boys could speak English, and they could help Hans. This would be a new school; it wouldn't be as difficult as it was when Alfred had to start all by himself without knowing a single word of the language. It pleased her to see how clean, happy and full of joy they all were as they left the house for the two-mile walk to the school. In the doorway Meta watched them with that strange feeling of an impending ill that she had so often experienced during the past three years in America, a feeling that was too often vindicated by the events which followed.

From the barn door, unobserved by the boys, their father watched them go down the road. He was a stern man in all things, but in nothing was he more exacting than in matters of education. He carried with him the educational ideals of Denmark, and in his innocence of the new world of Nebraska, he believed that education here was accorded the same honor and respect that was so familiar to him in the old country village. He had not learned much about the life on a Nebraska farm and he knew even less about the Nebraska country schools. All he knew was that the state gave free education, and that it was very democratic. A poor boy could go to the free schools and become a great man. He could even become President. Every emigrant was aware of that even before he came to America. It was a possibility which gave scope to the dreams that were all too soon dissipated in the grim reality of actual experience.

From the barn doorway he watched his three sons leave for school. He felt a proud, sad pain in his heart. He believed that his boys would be educated men in this new world; that here they would have the opportunities that Denmark could never have given them. He could not foresee the bitter struggle that would come—nor even understand the narrow hatred that at times covered his whole family with a cloud of deep despair. He glanced at the house and saw his wife with the two babies, one, a boy almost two years old, the other, a girl a year younger. He noticed that Meta was wiping her eyes. Quickly throwing some hay to the horses, he went to the house. He was going to say something about the boys, but all that came out was, "Why haven't you got the coffee ready?"

She saw that it was still a good hour and a half till coffee time, but she answered, "Oh, I had almost forgotten coffee this morning."

"Well, you know we can't get anything done till we have our coffee." And with that he walked out to the cob pile and brought in a box of cobs for the stove, something that he had scarcely ever before done for her.

When the coffee was on the table, they talked of the corn which would soon be ready for husking, and of how they needed another new horse. If they could only get another horse, they could borrow a wagon from the neighbors, and then it would be possible to put two teams in the field at shucking time. Alfred and David working together at one wagon could no doubt do as much as a full-grown man could do. Peter knew he could again go to Jacob Paulsen, but he hated to do that because he would have to pay almost a double price as had been the case in the spring.

"But won't the banker in Weeping Willow lend you money for horses?"

"No," said Peter. "He told me money was scarce

and that he could only let me have twenty-five dollars at eight per cent interest. But he is a fine man, very friendly. He shook hands with me and talked to me like an equal. They are not stuck up here, like the bankers in Denmark."

"But in Denmark you could have borrowed a thousand crowns at half that interest rate."

Then followed the silence which so often was the only answer to comparisons between their new home and the old country from which they had come. There, they had lived in a brick house, well made and comfortable. Here they lived in a grey, unpainted shack. In the old country village there had always been friends to visit a few steps from their own door, but here acquaintances were so far away that they saw them only a few times a year.

Frank broke the silence by saying, "New horse."

"That's right, Frank, a new horse for you," said Peter as he rose to go back to the barn. To Meta, he added, "I am glad the boys are getting started in school."

"Yes. I am glad too," said Meta as she held her baby girl close in her arms, and smiled at Frank who had entered so bravely into the conversation. Whenever Meta grew discouraged she had only to think of Margaret. So much seemed to depend upon Margaret. Her blue eyes and long yellow curls were a promise in this new land. It meant that God had smiled on them, that God had listened to their earnest prayers.

4

Alfred and David talked a great deal to each other as they walked along the road on their way to school. They knew some of the boys in the neighborhood by sight, but they had never played with any of them. They had not had time for play, but they had seen the boys at times, mostly when they passed by on the way to the swimming hole in Weeping Willow Creek. They were also quite sure that they knew the ones who had broken their watermelons. Thus most of their information led them to dislike the children of the Nebraska farmers and also to fear them.

Hans listened but said very little. He had heard so much about all the good things of school that it seemed to him that it must be one of the most wonderful things in the world to be able to attend. It would probably be something like going to town only much better, because you could stay all day and then go back again the next day and again the day after that. He was very proud of his fine blouse, his nice shoes and his red dinner pail. Lost in his own thoughts, he was already imagining all the things he would have to tell his mother when the day would be over. He was six and a half years old and nervously excited about learning to read. He would soon have books that were all his own. There was no end to all that one could learn in school.

These pleasant reveries persisted until they topped the last hill and saw the schoolhouse before them. As they walked across the grounds they were greeted by a group of boys waiting at the schoolhouse door. It was always an event to have a new boy appear at school, but here were three of them. These boys had heard of the Grimsen family. They knew they were foreigners and that alone was enough to create a very unfavorable impression.

"Hello," said one of the boys.

Alfred and David answered, but continued toward the step leading to the schoolhouse.

"Wait a minute can't you? You're not in a hurry are you?"

"What's your name?"

"Are you brothers?"

"Who is the baby with the curls?"

"Look, he carries a tobacco box. Give me a smoke will you, kid?" and one of the boys grabbed at Hans' lunch pail. He was astonished, and only by swinging it into his other hand did he succeed in preventing the boy from grabbing it. The other children all carried their lunch in half-gallon syrup pails from which the labels had been removed, hence the scorn they expressed at Hans' red tobacco box which bore the name of the tobacco it had contained. This box had been Hans' prize possession for over a month. It was closely associated with all of his pleasant imagining about the happiness he would find at school.

Before the boy who had grabbed at his pail could make any further trouble for Hans, one of the older boys walked up to Alfred and said, "Can't you talk? Can't you tell us your name?"

"I'll talk when I want to," said Alfred.

"Oh, you will, will you? Well, take that," and he hit him square on the nose. In an instant the two of them were on the ground rolling in the dust. Alfred's white shirt was torn and bloody.

"Hit him, Jim."

"Hit the bastard."

"He's a damn Dane."

But Alfred was strong, and before long he was on the top pounding Jim in the face with all his might. The victory was his for the moment. When the other boys saw that Jim was losing the fight, one of them rushed to his aid. He kicked Alfred in the ribs just under the heart. For an instant Alfred sat as if paralyzed and then fell over on his side. Jim now came out from under and began beating the almost fainting boy, and again he was cheered by the others. At this moment the teacher appeared, ringing the bell. She inquired about the cause of the fight, and Hans listened with wonder while one of the big boys told how Alfred had started it. When David protested, the teacher told him to keep still, and ordered all of them into the school.

Then began the morning ritual of Bible reading, followed by singing " 'Way Down upon the Swanee River." Hans sat in wonder, almost ready to cry as he looked at his brother's pale face from which all blood stains had not yet been washed away. He stared at the blackboard where the motto for the day was copied in red and green chalk. The colors alternated for each letter. This combination of colors seemed very beautiful and drew his attention from the unpleasant moments that had just passed. He studied the words which he could not read:

That truth will prevail should encourage us in our trials.

After the singing was over, the books were brought out and assignments made for the day, and then the classes began. At last it was Hans' turn. There were four other boys and two girls who were in school for the first time. When they were seated on the bench in the front row, the teacher gave them books and began teaching them the alphabet. She was tall, middle-aged, and dressed in gray calico. As she talked she seemed to roll her upper lip back from her teeth so that she showed ugly, pale-red gums. Finally she said, "Who can recite a poem?"

No one answered.

"Can't any one of you say even a short poem?"

Hans was filled with fear. It seemed as though some terrible calamity had suddenly fallen upon all of them. It was like a deep conviction of sin. Again the teacher looked them over, and again she said, "Not one of you can recite a poem?"

Hans stood up and said, "I can." Then nervous with pride and fear, for the teacher's words had attracted the attention of the whole school, he spoke:

> *Den lille skorstenfejer dreng,*
> *Ma tidlige up fra sin varme seng. . . .*

Before he could go further the whole room burst into laughter. Confused and ashamed, he sat down. The teacher quieted the room, and then with more gentleness than she had yet shown, told him that he must not talk in a foreign language, that he must recite in English. This ended the period before recess.

He had learned his first lesson and that was that the language he used at home when he spoke to his mother, when he said all the things he liked best to say—the language he loved to speak was something to be laughed at in this Nebraska school. Even his brothers seemed ashamed to think that he did not know better than to recite that poem. Yet only the Sunday before he had recited all of it to the guests that had been at their home and all of them said he was a smart boy to memorize such a long poem.

Hans' brothers went out to play, but he stayed in the room at his desk. Not one tear did he allow to escape from his eyes filled almost to overflowing. He seemed old to himself. He seemed to have long, long thoughts of things past, of great hopes and unspeakable indignities. He thought of his mother, of Massachusetts, of the day when his brother David had begun school at Hampton. Even then he had wanted to go. If he could only keep quiet now he felt that he could forget the awful sorrow of this day. The alarm clock ticked away the minutes. He knew that when the big hand reached six it would be time for the other children to come in again. Painful as it was to have them around him it would be better than this battle with sad, silent thoughts. No words would do here—only silence, a silence that screamed in his ears, and echoed in the beating of his heart. His hands were folded just as he folded them every night when he prayed at his father's bed, but now they were pulled taut as a knotted rope. Suddenly his imagination called up the picture of Sam, the negro boy in Massachusetts. He saw him hang by his neck in the top barbed wire of MacBride's fence. He heard his awful screams and saw the red blood spurting from the severed left jugular vein. And then he saw Sam's father leap straight over the stone fence on the opposite side of the road. He saw him lift the bleeding boy from the tangled wire. Somehow this changed things. It quieted his nerves as the children filed back into the room.

The period up till noon was even pleasant at times— although strange. He saw one of the boys making queer signs which he didn't understand to a moronic child of sixteen who had been going to the school for years and was still in the fourth grade. He saw Hank Kirkman chew tobacco and spit in an empty ink bottle, a practice he varied occasionally by spitting defiantly through the open window. The teacher knew better than to interfere with him. He was twenty years old and came to school only for a month in the fall before corn-shucking time and another month or so in the winter. For six years this had been his regular practice. He was admired by the smaller boys for his ability to invent all sorts of deviltry.

Hans knew of him even before this day when he

saw him for the first time, and he knew that it would not do to cross him in any way. He was the terror of all the boys, the bully and the boss of the playground.

When noon came all the boys got their dinner pails and sat together on the front porch. Hans found himself opposite the great body of Hank. But he did not feel nervous about that, for all his thoughts had now turned to his lunch. He was suddenly hungry and he thought of the good things his mother had put in his dinner pail. A great longing, a homesickness almost choked him as he opened the little red box and lifted out the first piece of bread on which there was a fine slice of chicken. He felt a longing for his little brother and sister who would now be sitting at the table with his mother. It seemed as though he had been away from them for a long, long time. He remembered the clean yellow oilcloth that covered the kitchen table, and all the friendly comforts of the stove, the cat, and his dog, Bounce. For a moment it almost seemed as though he was eating there with them, but before he could take a bite Hank spoke to him.

"Say, kid, did you ever try the flying jump?"

He was so startled he could not answer.

"Answer, damn you, answer me!"

"No," came in a soft, low voice.

"Well, come here and I'll show you so that you'll know more than you do now before you eat."

Hank took him by the hand and led him from the porch to the playground. All the other boys held their positions without a movement, for they knew what would follow. Hank stretched himself flat on his back with his arms extended back over his head along the ground, parallel, palms upward. He then made Hans stand on the palms of the outstretched hands and lean forward to place his chest on Hank's upraised feet bent back to meet the body of the little boy. Then with a wild cry, Hank, by using both hands and feet, threw the boy high in the air. He landed on his face on the hard ground of the yard, twenty feet from where Hank, now in a sitting position watched the success of his trick.

"By God, that was a pretty one, wasn't it, boys?" To which they all gave their assent except Hans' brothers who had run over to him. He lay, partially stunned, bloody and crying in the dust. One eye was already swollen and blood was streaming from his nose. His blouse of which he had been so proud in the morning was covered with dirt and blood, to which were now added stains from vomiting. The boys picked him up and David decided to take him home. As they started off the yard, Hans asked for his dinner pail. This Alfred brought. Clinging to it, bleeding and crying, he started the long two-mile walk home.

When they had walked a mile they stopped by a creek to wash his face and hands. Hans had stopped crying, but at intervals his body shook with deep convulsive sobs. At last the long walk came to an end. They turned into the path by the cottonwoods and came to the kitchen door where their mother saw them standing, David trying to smile as though nothing was wrong, but Hans once more in tears as he heard his mother's voice and the Danish words that meant release from the awful experience of the first day in school.

IV

META WAS so busy in the kitchen that she scarcely had time to glance out the window at the two big corn-cribs. There was something unusual going on today. Anyone could see that. Here it was only three o'clock in the afternoon, and David had already unhitched one team and put it in the barn. He was now doing the same for the team that was hitched to his father's wagon. Alfred in his wagon was shoveling corn into the round slat-crib from the one wagon while his father was doing the same from his on the opposite side. On the top of the corn-crib sat Hans piling the corn that was thrown to him into a fine, high peak. He had estimated the slope to the peak just exactly right, for there were only a few bushels left in the wagon and they would finish the pile to an even, high point.

This was the end of corn-shucking. It was the seventh day of December, and Peter Grimsen with the help of his two oldest sons had shucked all of his "hundred" acres of corn. The two cribs contained two thousand and seven hundred bushels. It had been a long hard season. For thirty-six days, working Sundays and holidays, they had been at this task. Every morning they were in the field before dawn. Many a day they stood stamping their feet on the frozen ground waiting five or ten minutes until it would be light enough to see the corn ears. At night after dark they shoveled the last of their loads into the crib. More experienced corn-shuckers could have completed the task in much shorter time, but what they lost in speed they gained in persistence.

On Thanksgiving Day Meta had roasted two large roosters. She stuffed them with prunes and with them she served baked squash, potatoes and cabbage that had been cooked for twenty-four hours until it was a delicious dark brown color. She also made apple cake with well-browned bread crumbs, and for this occasion, served it with whipped cream. Peter grumbled a little at the extravagance of whipped cream, but he didn't really say much. It was too good. It was the best dinner they had eaten in their Nebraska home. Peter even said, "This is the best meal I have had in America," and then as if out of respect for the day, he added, "I wish that every suffering soul in the world could have as good a dinner today."

David and Alfred had expected their father to declare a half-holiday. It was of course unreasonable to have a whole day free as other people had, but the afternoon—that would be different. Counting on the afternoon off they had worked unusually hard in the morning and brought in twenty-five bushels. Sure enough—when they were through with dinner, their father said, "Alfred, you and David may put your team in the barn," and then before they could express their joy, he added, "We'll all three go out with my wagon and shuck just one load."

When Meta saw how utterly sad the boys seemed, she spoke up. "Peter, can't you all quit just this one afternoon? You know how hard you have worked."

"Yes, I know that. I also know that it may snow any day now, and that we have at least six hundred bushels of corn left in the field. We can have no peace till that is safely in the crib. Do as I say, boys."

It was done as Peter ordered on that day, but now the end had come. There had been brief snow flurries for the past two days, while today there was a sharp unsteady wind from the northeast that indicated a real storm. "Let it come now," said Peter as they threw up the last ears by hand that had been spilled on the ground. "Let it snow, we have our corn in the crib," he said to himself as he put up a ladder for Hans to use in climbing down. The boys all hurried to the kitchen, for they knew Meta was making something special for them, but they were hardly prepared for what they saw. There on the middle of the table stood a huge bowl of *aebleskiver*, while at the stove Meta had a large kettle of batter, and from her *aebleskive pande*, which she had brought with her from Denmark, she was turning them out seven at a time.

"Today you will have all you can eat," said Meta, "and if you get started now you won't have to spare the butter—at least not until your father comes in." They needed no urging. Plateful after plateful disappeared along with big cups of steaming coffee. Even Bounce and Hobson got their fair share. The children never overlooked their two dogs. Dewey had been given away to the Nielsen boys, because Peter said two dogs were enough for him to feed.

"How many did you eat, David?" said his mother.

"Twenty-five."

"All right, then you can call your father." But that was not necessary, for as Meta spoke he came through the door. He paused for a moment to look back at the full corn-cribs, as if he hated to close the door and shut them from his sight. "What a land, what a land," he said as with something like a sigh he closed the door.

2

The winter snow had held off longer than usual. There had been snow for Christmas, but no real severe storm until late in January. Then as if to make up for lost time it came with double fury. For three days a blizzard raged over the land. It drifted snow to the roof of the barn, it covered the hog shed, it sifted through the windows into the house so that whole bushels of it had to be swept up in the morning and carried outside. The dogs crouched in fear by the stove and could hardly be driven outside.

The first day of the blizzard it was possible to struggle through to the barn to perform the ordinary chores. Peter even lead the horses to the water trough and succeeded in the middle of the day in getting to the neighbors for drinking water.

He had planned to build some sort of a shed for his

two cows and three young heifers, but the storm had come before he could get time to do this. Now they stood by the shelter of the straw stack and shivered in the cold. "What shall we do with the poor cows?" said Meta. "They will freeze to death in this weather."

"I don't know what to do," was Peter's only answer. But that afternoon when he returned with the water, and saw that it had frozen almost solid, he knew that something must be done. With the boys' help he fought through blinding snow and carried armful after armful of straw into the chicken house. They then led the three young heifers into this shed which was barely five feet high. The chickens were frightened and flew around in great commotion, but Peter closed the door on them, feeling sure that all would be well as soon as the calves quieted down. For the two milk cows he hollowed out a deep shelter in the south side of the straw stack, and that was the best he could do for them.

The first day had been mild compared to the second. The house shook with the force of the wind. It was as though no wall could have kept out the cold. When Peter opened the kitchen door a blind darkness of wind and snow almost choked him. "We'll have to wait till afternoon, before we try to go to the barn," he said. Everyone in the house wore his winter coat and one person was kept busy almost continuously putting cobs in the stove. For cooking purposes, and for drinking water, panfuls of snow were melted. From a little lean-to at the side of the house, with a hole opening into the kitchen the cobs for the fire were easily available, although so much snow had drifted through the cracks that they were not entirely dry.

Noon came with no abatement of the storm. There were moments when it seemed as if the wind had quieted, but each lull was only followed by a more furious blast of the wind. It was as though some giant had grasped the door and was shaking it as if he would tear it from its hinges. In the house at midday it was so dark that the lamp had to be lighted. Everyone in the house was solemn with fear. Peter paced the room continuously with his hands behind his back. Every few minutes he would go to the window and try to peer through it as though he thought something might have happened to remove the heavy coating of ice from the inside and the drifted snow that lay piled against the outside of the window. At three o'clock he said, "Mother, I must get out to the stock. I am going to catch hold of the clothesline and follow it from the corner of the house to the post. I'll then cut it off, carry it with me to the barn, if I can find the barn. If I can't I'll at least be able to find my way back to the house."

When an hour had passed, and Meta was almost frantic with fear, Peter stumbled in at the door. He had succeeded in reaching the barn, where he had been able to fill the horses' mangers with hay, but beyond that he had not dared to go. If the cows should freeze to death, he could not help it.

That night the family did not dare to go to bed. All their bed blankets were brought to the parlor where they wrapped themselves as closely as they could and sat around the stove through the long night. Meta made coffee for all of them at midnight, but most of the time she sat by the stove with Margaret in her arms, fearing more for her than for any of the others.

When dawn came, the worst part of the storm was over. By noon the wind had almost ceased to blow, and a brilliant sun shone over rolling, smoking drifts of white snow. Each building looked like a great round mound of snow. There was hope again. Peter and the boys began to clear a path to the barn.

"First dig your way to the straw stack," said Peter. "I am afraid that no animal could have lived through this storm, but we have to find out for certain."

Alfred and David worked together with their shovels, and before an hour had passed they had dug to the two cows, almost buried in the straw stack. Their shouts of joy at finding the cows alive reached Peter in the barn. He came running to see for himself. "Now, boys, take handfuls of straw and rub them from head to foot until you get every bit of snow out of their hair, and then get the pails and milk them."

They set to work with a will and with such good results that by the time they had finished the cows were eating the hay which Peter had brought them. David ran to the house for the milk pails. Alfred sat down by the new cow, known as White Back, while David started with Old Red. David had no sooner seated himself and begun stroking the udder to clean

off the snow and straw that still clung there till he
noticed that one of the front teats seemed terribly stiff.
He took it between the palms of both his hands and
began to rub it gently, thinking to soften it, when to his
horror it came off at the base as an icicle will snap
from the board to which it is attached. This was more
than David could stand. He began to cry and ran to
his father holding the frozen teat in his hand. Old Red
went on eating hay as though nothing had happened.
When Peter arrived, he saw that only one of the teats
had been frozen badly enough to break off. He now
gently massaged the whole udder until the milk began
to flow.

Old Red had been permanently injured for that
year. Since she was to come fresh in March it was almost time for her to be dried up. This proved to be a
fortunate circumstance, since it gave her udder time
to heal. She became a three-teat, but gave as much
milk as ever after her next calf was born. But at the
time, it loomed as one of the major tragedies of the
storm. For David it was a nightmare experience long
remembered.

There were too many things to be done before darkness came to give time for brooding. Fence posts were
brought to prop up the straw roof of the hollow in the
stack that had been further enlarged. Then other
posts were braced on the outside and the loose straw
that had been dug out was piled against these posts
until only an opening the size of a narrow barn door
remained. The calves were then brought down from

the chicken house and placed in this improvised straw shed along with the two cows. Since the opening was to the south this little shed was as warm and snug as Peter's own parlor. The calves were given warm skimmed milk brought from the house, but the horses and cattle could not be watered that day. The drifts on the creek were so deep that it would be impossible to reach the water. Each horse's grain box was filled with snow and there was so much snow on the hay that they did not seem to suffer from the want of water.

The chicken house was completely banked with snow. It seemed fairly snug. It was quite clear that some of the hens had had their toes frozen off, but all of them ate of the corn that Alfred scattered on the ground for them, after he had raked the straw to one side. By the time darkness came everything was in order once more. The kitchen was warm and cheerful. The snow piled high around the house kept away the drafts and since the wind had gone down, it had been possible to keep the house warm. Even Meta seemed cheerful although neither she nor any one else could forget the accident to Old Red. Peter blamed himself, for he believed that had he noticed the condition of her udder, he might have saved the frozen teat.

All the bedding had been carried back to the various beds and the kitchen table was set with steaming bowls of buttermilk soup, thickened with oatmeal and enriched with cooked prunes. A large plate of fried salt pork stood in the middle of the table, and beside it huge stacks of brown bread. This was a combination of foods that never failed to bring shouts of joy from the boys. They ate the bread and pork with the soup. At least three bowls were consumed by each of the older boys before they were satisfied. Bounce and Hobson had a rich dish of their own in which all the pork rinds were mixed.

Everyone retired early to make up for the loss of sleep the night before, everyone except Meta. She sat by Margaret's cradle, a box that had been moved into the parlor the night before on account of the cold. Margaret had shown signs of a cold all day, and now in the night she developed a peculiar choking cough. It did not seem very bad. "Even if it should be whooping-cough, the other children have had that. That is nothing to worry about," said Meta to console herself.

3

Margaret had whooping-cough, but it seemed to be a very light case. For the first week she scarcely choked at all when she coughed. Then one Saturday morning while Peter was getting ready to go to town, she suddenly developed a spell of coughing that lasted for over ten minutes and was accompanied by severe choking. It finally ended in vomiting. Both Meta and Peter were frightened. They decided immediately that Peter should ask the doctor to come out to see Margaret.

The roads had by this time been cleared sufficiently to make driving possible. The horses could not move

faster than a slow walk. The seven miles to Weeping
Willow had never seemed so long as they did this cold,
winter day.

It was an hour past noon before Peter Grimsen
reached the doctor's office. The waiting-room was open
and a sign hung on the locked door of the inner office.
This sign was a note scribbled with a pencil. Peter
could make nothing out of it, but he waited for an
hour, thinking the doctor would return. "It beats all
how short a winter day can be," he said aloud. "I had
better do my trading and return." Acting upon his own
advice, he went to the store, completed his shopping,
and again returned to wait. In the meantime he had
gotten one of John Hansen's boys to go to the office to
read the sign. From him Peter learned that the doctor
would not be home until late in the afternoon. There
was only one thing for Peter to do. He asked his friend
the grocery man to tell the doctor to come out to the
farm. Hansen promised that he would be sure to watch
for the doctor's return and give him the message.

Peter did not reach home until long after dark. He
found Meta almost frantic with fear and the exhaustion
of watching and waiting for the doctor. Shortly after
Peter left, and long before he could even have reached
town, she began watching the road for the appearance
of the doctor's buggy. "He may come at any time," she
said. Was it not possible, she reasoned that Peter might
have met him on the road somewhere. She tried to
make herself believe in such a possibility, but all the
time she knew how very improbable it was.

The long afternoon passed and darkness shut out the view of the road. No doctor came—not even Peter. At seven o'clock, when he did come to tell his story, Meta became sick with fear. Her face was drawn with pain and her eyes shifted from one part of the room to another in her impotent anguish. The big bed in which she and Peter slept had been moved into the parlor, during the day in order that Margaret might be kept warm. She lay pale and weak, her small delicate face framed in a mass of golden curls.

Even Peter could not eat supper that night in spite of the wearisome day he had spent. He drank two cups of hot tea, and also persuaded Meta to drink a cup. Every few minutes she went to the door where she listened for the sound of buggy wheels.

For the tenth time she asked, "Do you feel sure that Hansen will not forget?"

"Meta, I am sure he will remember. Why, sometimes on a Saturday he has a message for almost everyone that comes into the store, and he remembers them all. Today I heard him tell Lars Hansen that a man over from Alvin wanted Hansen to come and get the pigs that were now weaned from the sow. If he can remember such things, don't you believe he can remember that our little girl is sick?"

"But did you tell him that Margaret was very sick?" This was the third time she had asked that question.

Peter answered again as he had each time before. Nine, ten, and then eleven o'clock came. Peter walked up the road to the corner a mile away. At almost each step he stopped to listen for the sound of a buggy on the road. At the cross-roads he stood for half an hour waiting. It was very cold.

Meta watched Margaret and saw that she did not sleep. Her yellow curls gleamed in the pale lamp-light, framing her beautiful, flushed and feverish face. The coughing spells came often now, and each spell ended in vomiting. Outside the wind had begun a dismal, wintry whistling noise as it flew around the corners. Margaret's eyes pleaded for help. Since late in the afternoon she had not spoken a word. Her look seemed to be one of wonder that her mother could not help her. The hours dragged on. Twelve, one o'clock and Peter was back again. Meta knelt by the bed and prayed God to spare her little daughter. She told God how much she needed her in this lonely land so far away from Denmark and home.

Nothing seemed to help Margaret's cough. Meta rubbed her chest with a warm mixture of lard and turpentine, but no matter what she tried it gave the child no relief. Meta's efforts had only one reaction; they increased her own sense of futility and despair. If they could only know when the doctor would come, or even be sure that he had gotten their message from Hansen, it would have relieved their anxiety to some extent.

At last Peter decided that he would have to go back to town. Meta made him a cup of coffee, while he went out to harness the horses and give them a feeding of grain. On his way back to the house he heard a team coming down the road. He rushed into the house to tell Meta.

It seemed as though new life had been born in them. For a moment, they believed that at last all their troubles would be over. They had waited so long for the doctor, that they had come to believe he could work miracles.

In a few minutes he arrived. Peter was at the door to take care of his horses while he went directly into the house. Meta, who, at times, believed that she could express herself in English, found that in dealing with the unfamiliar words needed to describe Margaret's sickness, she could say nothing.

The Doctor, however, understood that it was a case of whooping-cough. He went to the bedside as soon as he had warmed his hands. It was quite clear to him that the baby was very sick. As soon as Peter came in, he explained that there was only one thing that could be done. He wanted to place the baby in a tub of ice cold water in which there was to be a generous mixture of mustard. He asked Peter to explain this to Meta.

"In cold water, Peter! Can he really mean that he wants to put her in ice cold water?"

"Yes, that is what he says."

"Oh, Peter, that means she will die. How can he tell us to take that poor, little thing out of her warm bed and put her in a tub of cold water? Let's not do it, Peter. Oh, it is too terrible a thing to do. Why should I be made to hurt my child that I have never willingly allowed to suffer even a blast of cold air, and now I am asked to place her in cold water. I can't do it. It is too awfully cruel."

Peter tried to explain to the doctor, who in turn told him that it was their only chance to save the child's life. As they talked she began again another fit of coughing and choking. It seemed as though she would die before anything could be done.

"He says we must do it, Meta."

She did not answer, but went to the kitchen to bring in the wash tub. It was then partly filled with water. A small package of mustard was dissolved in a bowl and poured into the tub.

"Now, tell your wife to undress her and place her in the water," the doctor instructed Peter.

"He says you must undress her and place her in the water."

Meta's hands shook as she undressed her child and lifted her in her arms. Margaret clung to her mother. She put both her small arms around her mother's neck and pressed her soft curls against her mother's face. Her coughing had ceased. It was as if she knew her mother would save her and ease her pain.

"Oh, Peter, is there no other way?"

Peter looked at the doctor, who answered by saying, "Tell her to do it now while the baby is not coughing."

"You must do it, Meta. He says you must do it now while the baby is not coughing."

Meta knelt by the tub and slowly pulled her baby's hands from around her neck. She placed her in the water. Margaret struggled and screamed, "Mama,

Mama." Then her head fell to one side. There was a sudden convulsion and she was dead. Meta picked her quickly from the water. Even the doctor got excited and helped to massage the child, but after a couple of minutes, he said, "It is no use."

Meta fell to her knees by the bed and buried her face in the pillow by her daughter. "Margaret, Margaret," she said very softly. "Do you know, Margaret, that I loved you? You didn't believe I was punishing you? Did you, Margaret? Tell me, Margaret, oh, tell me you knew I was not punishing you. Oh, Margaret, tell me you knew I loved you. Just tell me that, Margaret, before you go."

The doctor began to gather up his things. He put on his coat. Going over to the bed he straightened the legs of the dead child, crossed her hands on her breast, and then placed a penny on each eyelid to weigh them shut forever. They were like monstrous blemishes on the pale face surrounded by light-gold curls.

He tapped Peter gently on the shoulder, "I am afraid that is all I can do. It's now already daylight. I must hurry away. Hansen forgot to tell me till after he closed his store and that was not till midnight, because it was Saturday. I must be going. Good-bye."

Peter did not lift his head. He sat bowed in a chair. "Yes," he said, "Yes," he repeated sometime later when he heard the doctor drive out of the yard. "Yes, that is the way it is with us, now."

The sun rose striking brilliant beams of light across the snow-covered land and through the partially frosted windows. The lamp burned on, a pale yellow flame showing through a soot-coated chimney. Meta and Peter stayed as they were until Alfred came down to find his little sister with copper pennies weighing down her eyelids.

4

Many of the neighbors were very kind. One of them came to help Meta with the washing. Another came and offered his three-seated spring wagon for the funeral. On the day Margaret was buried two neighbors came to follow in their own buggies the three-seated spring wagon in which the Grimsen family rode. They were all in the one wagon. Margaret's coffin occupied the back seat.

She was buried in the Weeping Willow graveyard, but not in the part which was gardened. There the space was too expensive. She was buried in the rough uncultivated space where rested all the poor; where they slept the unwaking sleep under plain board markers.

5

One morning a month later Peter noticed that the picture on the calendar had been cut away. "What happened to the calendar, Meta? Have the children been cutting it to pieces?"

"No," answered Meta in such a sharp tone that Peter wondered, but said nothing. She did not tell him that part of her tragedy was that she had never had Margaret photographed. The picture on the calendar reminded her somewhat of her daughter, so she had cut it out and put it away in a hiding place of her own where it now lay with a lock of Margaret's yellow curls tied into one corner of the picture.

V

"DEAR MOTHER:

"Alfred will read this letter to you, and tell you everything I write. Today we listed eight acres. It was all half-mile rows. That is why we got so much done. My drill is not very heavy, but the bolt is rusted where the handles could be let down. That's why they are so high that I have to reach up all the time. My arms get so tired that I can't think sometimes. Then I just have to stop and shake them. But Alec says I mustn't stop, because he wants me to keep up with him all the time. Sometimes the drill is hard to turn at the end of the rows. Alec gets mad if I don't start straight at the end of each row. Eight acres is twenty miles long."

David paused and stared out of the window. It was so quiet in the house that he was just a little frightened. It was so different from his own home where there was always someone around. He had been hired out by his father to drill corn for Alec Smith. He was to get twenty-five cents a day. At first he had been very glad to become a real hired man. He was now ten years old which really made him feel quite grown up. There weren't many boys who could do a man's work at ten. He felt very sure of that. It had made a big impression on the other boys at school when he told them he was staying out of school to work as Smith's hired man.

He felt very lonesome, because it was Sunday and Mr. and Mrs. Smith had gone to visit a neighbor. They told him that he should write to his mother and that their neighbor would take the letter over on Monday. Peter Grimsen had bought two milk cows from this man, and he was to deliver them the next day. David heaved a great sigh and began again.

"Last night I had to do four rows, that's two miles, after Alec unhitched. You see I always have to be four rows behind him, because the horses on the lister couldn't pass my horse if I were only two rows behind. He said that because it was Saturday night I had to finish up. It might rain and wash the loose dirt away, he said. I didn't know that, and it was so hard to start back up those long rows after he went home. But I rode my horse home after I finished.

"I keep the camphor you gave me right by my couch. I sleep on the couch in the parlor. When I wake up and my knees ache I just rub them like we do at home and then I can go to sleep again. But last night I didn't wake up when it hurt, for Alec came and hit me so hard with a yardstick that it left welts on me and said that if I didn't stop screaming in my sleep, he would give me something to scream for when I was awake. And then I cried because he had hurt me so much, but more because my knees hurt and it didn't seem like the camphor could help my knees much. Alec was awfully mad, but it wasn't my fault was it, mother, if I didn't even know I was screaming?"

He paused again. It was three o'clock. They would be having coffee at home now, and Hobson and Bounce would be there. And his mother would be wearing a clean dress. Everything in the kitchen would be so tidy and comfortable. Then after coffee, the boys might go out to the horse pasture or to their secret cave in the prairie. He picked up his pencil and continued the letter.

"Mother, don't you think Dad would let me come home next Saturday night? I could walk part of the way, and Hans could ride Prince to meet me and then we could easily ride double the rest of the way home. My shoes get so full of dirt that my feet hurt all the time. I don't see how I can stay here two more weeks without coming home. How many pigs did the red sow get?"

And then he stopped for he realized that if he were to enquire about all the things he would like to know at home, he would be writing all day. He signed his name, "David," folded the letter, put it in an envelope and wrote on the outside "To my Mother."

2

Mrs. Smith was kind to him, and praised him for the letter he had written, although she did not ask to read it, to David's great relief. "I'll watch for Eli Day tomorrow and when he passes I'll give your letter to him."

"When do you think he will get back?" said David.

"It may be evening before he returns, because he is going on to town after he leaves your father's place."

"Then maybe I won't know if he has a letter from home for me."

"You can go over to his place after chores tomorrow night."

Monday was another long day in the field. After work there was always the chores. David had to milk three cows, feed the calves, carry in cobs, and help Mrs. Smith with the dishes after supper. It was eight o'clock and already dark before supper was over that night. He had hurried so much that he was almost sick, and he could scarcely eat any supper. Mrs. Smith saw how worried he was, and said that he might go if he liked. That she would leave the dishes for him to wipe after he came home.

It was only a mile to the Eli Day's place. When he got there the family was still at the supper table. He was a little scared of them, because he didn't know any of them.

"Hello, boy," said Mr. Day when he saw him through the screen door. "What can I do for you?"

"Did my mother . . ." and then he stopped because he saw that he could not say what he wanted so much to say. He had imagined somehow that when he saw Mr. Day, he would find out all sorts of things about home. There were a hundred things he wanted to hear about, and now he saw that he could not really ask any of the questions, he had asked aloud all day long as he followed the drill through the listed rows. "Did you give my letter to my mother?"

"Your letter? Oh, you are Grimsen's boy over at Smith's. By golly, sonny, I believe I forgot that letter. Let me see. Oh, it's in my jacket pocket out on the wagon. No, sonny, I forgot to give it to your mother. We had so much trouble getting the cattle into the barnyard that I forgot all about it."

"All right," said David, and turned away. He didn't even think to ask for his letter back again, or to go out to the wagon, where he could have found it crumpled and greasy in Mr. Day's jacket pocket. He turned and walked back to Smith's place. He was too tired and disappointed to cry. Sometimes a dry sob shook his whole body, but he did not cry.

That night he screamed again in his sleep, but Mrs. Smith heard him before her husband did. She got up and rubbed his knees with camphor until he was quiet again. He didn't even wake up or know that she had done that for him.

3

Trying to forget the unforgettable is to remember, and remember and remember. Meta did her best. If she could not forget, she could at least keep her bitter and sweet, sad memories to herself. There were so many things that could not be put out of mind: A little girl's dress on a clothesline, an old shoe of Margaret's that suddenly appeared as if it had come of its own account to say something for itself, a broken dish, uncovered by the melting winter snow, a bold robin sitting on the post by the corner of the house, a slow-moving wagon appearing over the crest of the hill, a piece of blue cloth, a lonely rag of a cloud tearing itself to pieces in a blue, spring sky; there are so many things that make trying to forget an instensified form of remembering.

There were so many things to do that spring. Meta planned to raise two hundred chickens. Every day when another hen got ready to sit she had a dozen well selected eggs to put under her. Soon there was a full row of twenty nests. Then began the hatching period. Early and late Meta cared for the chickens. There were finally almost two hundred of them. But the rats came. Every morning little bits of downy pieces of dead chicken were strewn over the chicken-house floor. Meta set traps, put poisoned wheat down the rat holes, locked the cats in the chicken house, but nothing could stop the loss of her chicks. Finally the boys built little houses for the brood hens out of boxes and placed them on a raised platform with little ladders reaching to the doors. They nailed tin around the legs that supported these houses and at night removed the ladders. This did the trick, but not until almost a hundred chickens had been lost.

Meta also planned a more extensive garden, but there were so many things to do that most of it grew to weeds. When she tried to transplant cabbage and kale the plants died, because she did not have enough water to keep the ground moist around them for a few days until the roots could take a new hold on the soil.

Every day she had to cook the milk for the calves, four of them. They had developed some form of diarrhea that only well-boiled milk could stop. It was also her duty to carry milk to the little pigs at noon. She did all the washing for her large family on a wash board, and no matter how much water the boys carried up from the creek, she never had enough to do the rinsing properly. She sewed shirts for the boys by hand, and she put endless patches on their overalls.

One day when Peter returned from town, he had a stranger sitting beside him on the seat. As soon as the wagon stopped in the yard she saw him go to a willow tree and cut off a small branch. "What is he doing, Mother?" said Hans.

"I don't know. I don't even know who he is."

"Can I go out and see?" He was peeling the potatoes for the evening meal.

"Yes, I guess I can finish the potatoes, and you can come back to tell me all about it. Will you do that?"

"You bet I will," and he disappeared like a flash out of the door. He started running toward the man, but decided that perhaps it would be better if he walked up to him with an air of not being too concerned. The man was cutting his willow stick in the form of a fork much like a slingshot brace.

Hans stood still watching him. He paid no attention to the boy, continuing with his whittling. Occasionally he would put his knife down on a branch of the tree and try holding his hands first one way or then another on the two forks of the stick. Suddenly he spoke in a very sharp, loud voice. "Do you know what this is, boy?"

"No," said Hans. Almost frightened by the man's voice.

"It's a water witch. Do you hear me? It's a water witch."

"A witch?" said Hans, glancing behind him toward the house to see that everything was still all right.

"Yes, a water witch."

"I wonder if he is trying to fool me," thought Hans. He looked again at the man. The more Hans looked at him the stranger he seemed to become. Maybe there was something queer about him. The man was now whittling again. He had a pocket knife with a blade that was almost as long as a butcher knife. Hans took a step or two backward and turned around. He wanted to walk slowly back to the house, but he couldn't hold his legs. He ran through the door. "You know what he is doing Mother? He is making a witch. That's what he said, a witch."

"Now, Hans, he must have been fooling you. What could he mean saying he was making a witch."

"Well, that's what he said."

"He was fooling you, Hans. Peter is coming now so we'll know what it's all about."

"Peter, who is that man you brought here with you?"

"That is a surprise for you, Meta. He is a well driller and he is going to drill a well for us."

"No, you don't say. Oh, my, but that will be nice. Can't we have it right here by the house, so that we won't have to carry the water very far?"

"I don't know. He says there is no use trying to drill unless the witch indicates water."

"Oh, now, I see what he meant about the witch. Hans said he was making a witch. It's a water witch, Hans. It tells you where there is water so that you can always be sure you are drilling in the right place. Do you believe there is any truth in that, Peter?"

"I don't know. It seems kind of funny, but I know he won't drill on any spot not marked by the witch."

They now watched him from the door as he walked slowly first in one direction and then another. He went by the corner of the barn, over to the hen house, and back to the tree again where he had made his water witch. He was holding it firmly in his two hands so that the end of the crotch was pointing toward his breast.

"Doesn't look like he was finding water," said Meta. "It looks like a lot of foolishness to me. Everybody around this part of the country has water, why shouldn't we have it here?"

"Yes, but he has drilled most of the wells, too, and he says his witch has never failed him."

He was now walking in the direction of the hog pen.

Just as he reached the fence the stick flew out of his hand into the pen.

"Now, that would be a fine place to have a pump," said Meta sarcastically. "If he can't do better than that he had better send his witch back to town, or wherever it comes from."

They now saw him climb over the fence, pick up a splinter of a board about a foot long and drive it into the ground at the exact spot where the water witch lay. "There's water here," he shouted in the direction of the house as he climbed over the fence into the yard again. He came up to the house. "Mr. Grimsen, you may have to move your hog pen, because that's the only place I seem to find water."

"But that's so far away. Can't you try nearer to the house?" said Peter.

"Oh, I can try but I don't think it will do much good. I have found that I get the best results where the witch points the very first time. It is not always good luck to try for a second place. You take my advice and drill right where that stick stands and you will be sure of water."

"Well, couldn't you try here by the house? I'd like to have the well right where we are standing."

"Maybe you would," he said rather sarcastically, "but you'll have to have it where there is water won't you? What is the use for me to drill in dry ground? Tell me that."

It was quite clear that he was not to be persuaded to change his opinion. Of all the inconvenient places for a well the one he had picked was the very worst. Peter hesitated. Meta looked worried, and very skeptical of everything the man was saying.

"You see how it is, Mr. Grimsen. If we don't drill where there is water what is the use of drilling at all? Now, I have been drilling wells in this country for near onto thirty years and I have never yet had a failure. And why? Because I never drill unless the water witch says there is water, that is why. I make my witch fresh each time, and then I hold it in my two hands just like this. I then bend them back, not too far, but just as I am doing now. That is the first thing to do. Then I look over the land and walk slowly. It is important to walk just right. Not too fast. It isn't everyone, by any means, for whom a water witch will work. You must take slow even steps like this." As he finished he took two steps and the witch flew out of his hands almost on the exact spot where Meta had wanted the well.

Hans jumped as if he had seen a snake. Meta turned into the house to conceal her amusement. Peter stayed because he saw his opportunity. "You see, there is water right here," he said.

The well driller looked a trifle nonplussed, picked up his stick, and said, "Yes, I guess there is. It may be a little deeper than it is out there, but there is water all right. Yes, you can have the well here if you want it, although I would advise you to put it out there. I think you would find water out there at the forty-foot level."

"Put it here," said Peter.

"All right, just as you say."

The well was drilled where Peter had desired it, and water was found at a depth of thirty-three feet. This well with a brand-new green pump was the great wonder of that year. For a long time it was almost a constant subject for conversation. The boys fought with one another for the privilege of pumping water for the horses, and Meta could scarcely ever get to try it for herself. She let them have their fun, for she knew that before very long she would have more than her share at the pump handle. Before the summer was over she often had to pump the trough full before the men folks came in from the fields at noon. Peter sometimes scolded and said she should not do it, but she could not bear to see the sweaty, tired horses trying to drink at an empty trough.

4

The well was only a small part of the improvements on the farm that year. Peter had increased his stock to the place where he needed more buildings, and he proceeded to get them. He was determined that his cattle would have a shelter for the winter. Thus before threshing time he built a large rough framework of logs over which he placed the straw stack when he threshed his grain. After the straw had settled, he dug a passageway to the door, cleaned out the loose straw that had settled through the framework, and his barn for the cows and young calves was the warmest, snuggest building on the whole farm. He bought lumber for an enlargement on his hog shed and even bought a window to put in the south side. Visitors praised it. They said it was more like a palace than a hog shed. He added a lean-to at the side of the barn to use for Kitty later on in the winter. Kitty had been bred to a stallion in Weeping Willow and would foal sometime in March. He had also put up one permanent corn-crib with a board floor to take the place of one of the slat-cribs. He did this because he wanted, if possible, to save one crib of corn for the spring or early summer when prices were usually higher than in the winter. The slat-crib with the corn on the bare ground was all right as long as it was shelled while the ground was still frozen.

Peter had paid for all these improvements. He had bought the material and done all the work with the help of his sons, all except the well. He had argued more than once with the landlord, but had never gotten a cent of help except for one thing; the landlord had paid for the pump and the thirty feet of pipe needed for the well. The expense of drilling and tiling the well Peter had paid. Everyone knew why the landlord had paid for the pump, for since it was not an attached fixture it could legally be moved away by the renter should he care to take it with him.

When winter came every animal was well housed. It was a pleasure to do the milking in the warm straw shed, or to stand in the passageway of the hog house with the door closed on a cold day and yet have plenty of good sunlight coming through the window. Even the house was warmer this winter, for Peter had built up a fence about two feet high around all sides of the house except the south, where the floor was level with the ground. This fence was built about three feet away from the sides of the house and the intervening space was filled with manure from the horse barn. Thus every possibility of a draft under the house was prevented.

Meta had watched all these careful preparations with great interest. She was happy to think that the poor cattle would not have to suffer again this year as they did last. But all the time she had some plans of her own, for in all this improving nothing had been done to the inside of the house. It was still the same ragged and dilapidated shack to which they had moved two years ago.

One day in January while Alfred was making out an order from the Sears and Roebuck Catalogue, Meta had interrupted him while he was writing the number of a four-tined pitchfork to say that she also had an order. Hans and David sat very tense on the opposite side of the table, because they knew what it was. Meta had gotten them to do the reading for her. They had figured the quantity and the price. Now the moment had come. They looked at their father.

"You, Meta, you have an order, too? Don't you think I have already had more expense on this place than I can well afford?"

"Maybe that you have, but none of it has been on the house."

"The house! What's the matter with the house? Aren't we comfortable here?"

"I am not. I want wallpaper for the parlor. I just can't stand those ugly bare walls any longer. You know there isn't another home we visit, no matter how poor the people are that does not have paper in the parlor at least. I am willing to leave the kitchen as it is, but I want the parlor papered."

Peter looked around him and was quiet. He could see how things were. Maybe he thought of other things, too, that Meta had endured in these rooms, for when he spoke again, he surprised the boys by saying, "What would it cost us, Meta?"

"Four dollars and twenty cents, and that includes the border, too," said David as quick as a flash.

Peter smiled. "So you are in on it, too, are you, David? Who else?" He looked around the table.

"Me. That's all," said Hans, with a sigh of relief that could be heard all over the room. He had been so very doubtful about this business that he had scarcely dared to breathe for the last half-hour. There were times when he had been afraid that his mother wouldn't even mention the subject in spite of all she had said to the boys, and picking out the exact paper, too.

"All right, Meta, you shall have it," said Peter.

"Thank you for that," she replied.

5

What joy and excitement there was in the house, the day the paper arrived! It was a vivid yellow with a

pattern of large pale-red roses. Meta was as excited as
the boys were. "I don't think I can even sleep until we
have it on the wall," she said. "Now we'll no longer
be living in a house that's more like a pig pen than a
place for Christian souls."

Everything was arranged to have the papering done
on the following day. Meta had scarcely started the
morning fire, before Hans came quietly down the steps
and into the kitchen.

"Why, Hans, what are you doing up so early?"

"I couldn't sleep. I guess I'm not feeling well
today."

"Not well? What's the matter?"

"I don't know. I believe I have a pain in the stomach."

As he talked, she saw him looking at the big stack
of wallpaper that lay on the kitchen bench.

"So that's it," she thought. "He wants to stay home
from school today to help with the papering."

"We'll soon have a cup of coffee, Hans, and then
we'll both feel better."

"Maybe, but I don't think so. I'm awfully sick."

"Yes, I know you are. I'm afraid your father won't
let you stay home from school, but maybe you could
get permission to come home at last recess. How would
that be?"

He thought for a moment and realized that that
was probably the best he could do.

"All right, mother, that's what I'll do. I'll come
home a-flyin', and don't you think David could come,

too, and that maybe we wouldn't have to say anything to the old man, 'cause he won't hardly notice that we are home early anyway? We could do all our lessons. . . . You know we *could* do them all by noon. The kids are so dumb that we are always through in less than half the time it takes them, and then we could save the whole noon hour. But then we'd have to tell the old man, wouldn't we? Oh, I guess we'll just come at last recess."

His mother let him ramble on. She had gone through plans like this before with Hans, and she knew that if she gave him time he would figure it out for himself. She also felt deeply for him, because she knew what a delight he got out of making something in the house. Never before had any of the boys seen paper put on walls. This was a treat, and one of the neighbors was coming down to help hang it.

At exactly two-thirty o'clock the boys were home.

"But how did you get here so soon? This is just recess time."

Hans answered quickly and in a low tone, "We made teacher think I was sick, and that David had to take me home."

Then David spoke. "Just after history class, which was about half-past one, Hans was to fall out of his seat and faint. He fell all right, but he did not faint. But he cried so hard the teacher came, and then I told her that Hans had been sick for days, and that I had better take him home. So she let us go."

Their mother said nothing more, for she knew that

they should have stayed at home in the first place. Their help was needed for trimming the paper, since it had come to them from the mail order house untrimmed. After a cup of coffee, all three of them went to work, trimming, putting on paste, and at other odd jobs. By nightfall the parlor was papered, ceiling and walls all complete.

It was a fairy-land of beauty to them. What a wonderful thing it was to sit by the stove and trace the rows of red flowers in every direction, crossways, diagonal, up and down. And then it was possible to divide these easily marked lines into still more complicated patterns and designs. It always worked out perfectly, no matter how you tried to prove it wrong.

That night, Meta served coffee in the parlor, and old Gus Marks and his son, Clyde, came down. Gus came "just to gas awhile" as he put it, but they all knew that he came to see the new wallpaper, for his son had known about it from school. He was the only one who was "in" on the sickness staged so successfully by Hans Grimsen.

Before the family went to bed, there were sounds of snapping and crackling in the paper.

"It seems to me that it should not crack quite so loudly," said Meta in a perturbed tone.

"Oh, yes," answered Peter. "It always does that when it's drying. It's well put on I know that. Now keep your chairs from the walls there, you kids. Do you want to tear the paper the first night it's on?"

After they had all retired, Meta kept hearing the

cracking from her bedroom until she feared something was wrong. But it had been a long, hard day, and she slept soundly till her usual winter rising time, about five o'clock. She always allowed herself the luxury of sleeping an hour or so later in the winter.

When she entered the parlor the first thing in the morning, a sorry sight confronted her. Instead of her beautiful parlor in yellow and red she saw a perfect shambles. Paper hung from the ceiling and from the walls in long shreds. It hung over the tables, chairs, and in front of the windows. It was as though some malicious fiend had worked diligently all night long to wreak havoc with her room. There was scarcely a square yard of paper unloosened or not completely fallen away.

Not until one of the boys came down at six o'clock was the kitchen fire started. Meta sat with her face hidden in her hands. She sat very erect and very quiet, but her manner seemed to imply that she had seen enough for that day. This, too, the new country had to do to her. In one little night the plans of many, many days had been ruined.

Peter said, "After all, it's only paper that is destroyed. It could have been worse, you know."

"I'm tired of trying to be satisfied by making myself believe that it could have been worse. I hate this place. Every inch of it is hateful to me. I have given it the best of my life, and all it has given me in return is sorrows without end. No one seems to have as hard a time as we do. Why can't we move to a place where we can have a decent house? Why do we have to stay in a place where the walls are so rotten they won't even hold wallpaper. Tell me that?"

But Peter did not answer her. He did not even mention the fact that he had spent four dollars and twenty cents for a thing of no utility, for a pleasure that now hung in miserable shreds from the walls and ceiling of his house.

VI

HANS AND DAVID had helped each other build a long
bench and fasten it to the side of the house next to the
kitchen door. On one end stood the wash basin and
over it was a roller towel-rack and a mirror. This was a
great saving for Meta, because from late spring to
early fall it kept all the spilled water around the wash
stand out of the kitchen. Not all of the bench was re-
served for this purpose. It was long enough to hold the
milk pails, and still leave space next to the door for a
seat. Here Peter and Meta often sat on summer nights
for an hour or so before bed time. When all the children had gone to bed it was a comfort to sit here and
watch the firebugs' endless tiny flashes in the
weeds down by the creek, or listen to the comforting
sounds of the cattle moving in the barnyard or hear
their heavy sighs as one by one they lay down before
beginning to chew their cud.

These quiet, restful moments also gave time to think
of the past and to plan for the future. Often as Meta
sat here with Peter and saw the darkness settle over
the waving fields of green corn, she wondered if her
children would have real underwear next winter, or
would they again have to walk out over those frozen
hills wearing an inner shirt made of a flour sack and
an extra pair of overalls for underwear. No, not if she

could help it they wouldn't. She shuddered over the many times when she feared they would not come home, and that they would be found frozen to death in some ditch in the field. "These are terrible things to imagine," she would think to herself. "I can certainly make things worse than they really are when I begin such speculations," she added half audibly in order to turn her mind to pleasanter thoughts.

Peter, too, had thoughts that were none too pleasant. He had carried his improvements a little too far the previous year. "God knows they were needed badly enough," he would console himself by thinking, but that didn't change the fact that by the time he had settled his bills, he faced the new season without a cent of cash to carry him through the summer and fall. He had held one crib of corn for higher prices, and had held it a little too long, so that he had been forced to sell for the same price that he could have had in December. This meant that the little extra he had planned above his debts was lost. He had already borrowed a hundred dollars from the bank, which he knew by experience marked the absolute limit in that direction. Eight per cent interest there, interest everywhere. "If it were not for that damnable interest we could all get along very well," he thought. Even the carriage and wagon shop where he bought his implements charged interest, only it was even worse than the bank, for the rate of interest there was a flat one per cent a month.

Night after night he would go over these same problems always seeking for a solution, hoping that there was a solution, and not understanding well enough the whole system under which he lived to know that there could never be a solution for him. The invisible chains that bound him were not so invisible but that he sensed their presence. What he did not know was that there could be no partial escape from his bondage, that for him and the millions who toiled in the black loam of this rich land there would be only one reality and that would be poverty—only this one truth as long as the system endured.

This early summer had been more promising than had ever been known to the mind of farmers in that region. The papers said it was the same in the whole Midwest region. In Illinois they talked of corn that would make seventy bushels to the acre. That sounded like boasting to Peter, but it seemed quite possible to him that his corn would make at least forty. He had some extra acres in small grain this year, which left him eighty acres of corn. But each day the price dropped on the Chicago market. The last report was that it had dropped to twenty.

Without preliminary warning or introduction he spoke out to Meta, "Even if it should only make forty, that would be over three thousand bushels of corn. And at twenty cents a bushel that would be around six hundred dollars, or better."

"Yes," said Meta, picking up the thread of his thought, "but it seems sad that the first year we have had any promise of a large crop that corn should be down to twenty cents."

"It may come up again. But how can we get through the summer without borrowing?"

Then Peter led around to the subject that he had wanted to discuss. A mile from their house lived Jacob Paulsen. Peter had gone to him for help before this and knew how much Meta hated to have any dealings with him, even though he was a Dane. He had come to this country before going to the Danish schools, and here he had never attended. He was known to all in Weeping Willow as one of the most ignorant men in the whole community. He could not even read the market reports in the newspapers, nor could he sign his own name to a check. His wife always had to write his checks and then he added a cross to her signature. In addition to his ignorance, he was a boaster and a braggart. In spite of his lack of education he was very shrewd in matters pertaining to money. His little sharp eyes shone in their fat pouches whenever there was a chance to make an extra dollar. Among his many operations, in addition to feeding cattle and farming, was lending money to new settlers at exorbitant rates of interest. A new settler could always buy horses and cows from him on credit, but they paid from two to three times what they were worth. They could also borrow money from him. His interest rate was two per cent a month.

Peter spoke again, "I could go to Jacob Paulsen, couldn't I?"

"Yes, but if you do, you know what that will mean."

"I have to get money somewhere. We haven't a cent

left and the grocery bill at John Hansen's is already sixty dollars. We must have a new cultivator, and another set of harness. I don't see what I am to do if I don't find someone who will lend me money."

"Well, go to Jacob then, and see if you can't borrow a little money."

The next day Peter walked up the road to Paulsen's place. When he reached the house he was astonished at the sight he saw. Here was the wealthiest farmer around Weeping Willow, and he used his front yard for a pig pen. Where the water spilled over from the pump and kitchen sink, the hogs had made a deep wallow which had completely undermined and destroyed the front steps. In place of steps, a plank with cleats nailed at regular intervals sloped up to the porch landing. Below this plank and under the porch, and around the well pipe lay about thirty hogs in a wallow of filthy, slimy mud and water. From this hog's paradise rose a nauseating stench. Inside the house, all was neat and clean, for Mrs. Paulsen was a fine housekeeper. It was said that she never invited guests to her home, because she was so ashamed of her front yard. Her husband was master and nothing she could say or do would force him to build a pen for his hogs away from the house. All he would say to her objections was, "It's cool for them here under the porch."

"Good morning, Peter," said Jacob, who was standing just inside the door watching Peter negotiate the precarious approach on his short, slightly bowed legs.

"Good morning. Your steps are a little hard to climb."

"Yes, but I got some damn fine hogs." Jacob now came out on the porch and assumed his characteristic position with his thumbs locked in the armholes of his vest. He guessed what Peter had come for, since no one ever came to visit him except on errands like the one that had prompted Peter. At such times, Jacob was in his element. He had his visitor in his power, and he knew that no matter how much he bragged and boasted he would not be contradicted. While Peter studied all the details of the hog wallow around the front porch, Paulsen talked of hogs. "My hogs always run around three hundred pounds when they are a year old. I always get a bigger price on the market than any one else. Last spring I shipped one car load to Omaha that brought me one thousand dollars. Most of my hogs bring about that much to a car. Right now, I have one hundred and fifty three-year-old steers about ready for the market. When I sell them I think I'll buy another farm. Why don't you buy the farm where you live? It's a good farm, ain't it? How much rent do you pay?"

"I pay a cash rent of four hundred and eighty dollars for the quarter section."

"Only four hundred and eighty? Why that's crazy. That farm is worth a half again as much as that."

"I don't believe so. Last year all my crops didn't bring me nine hundred dollars." As Peter spoke, he knew that he had made a fatal error. Now it would not be long until Jacob Paulsen would have the rent boosted on him. But that was not his business today.

"What I came for, Jacob," he hurriedly interjected, before Paulsen could start another long speech about how much money he made and how many farms he owned—"was to find out if, perhaps, you could make me a little loan."

"A loan? You a loan? Why a man that's renting a farm like you got for only four hundred and eighty dollars should have money to loan out."

Peter kept silent for a long time. Finally Jacob spoke again.

"How much do you need?"

"Three hundred dollars."

"Three hundred dollars! What in the name of hell do you need that much for? What are you going to buy?"

"I need more farm machinery and many other things," said Peter, in a tone that did not entirely conceal the resentment he felt toward Paulsen's insulting questions.

"Well, I tell you what I'll do."

"Now what deviltry can he be up to?" thought Peter to himself.

"You see, I was planning on buying a new farm this summer, and that would take all my cash balance. I don't believe I have more than ten or twelve thousand in the bank. But I never refuse help to a neighbor, so this is what I'll do to help you. I'll buy twelve hundred bushels of corn from you at twenty-five cents a bushel.

You are to deliver the corn in the Weeping Willow elevator before January first. And I'll give you the check this morning."

Peter felt a sickening sensation in the pit of his stomach. This was robbery and he knew it, for he was sure that corn would be at least thirty cents by winter. He did a rapid and easy calculation: five cents a bushel on twelve hundred would be sixty dollars. That would be twenty per cent interest for a five or six months' loan of three hundred dollars.

"No, Jacob, that I won't do. I would rather pay you two per cent interest a month as long as I have the loan."

"Two per cent a month, why, that's usury. I wouldn't think of asking that."

Peter understood him. He knew that Jacob always asked at least that much.

"No, I wouldn't treat a neighbor like that. Corn today is twenty-one cents. I'm offering you four cents over the market price."

"But you know that corn always goes up in the fall."

"Yes, and I know that it goes down, too. Only three years ago we sold corn for seventeen cents a bushel. This looks like a bumper year. I am just trying to help you. I am giving you a fair price."

And so that deal was closed. As Peter walked home he felt that he had been robbed again. "But still," he thought, "if I should raise three thousand bushels this year I'll have almost two thousand to sell at whatever the price may be."

Meta also was disturbed, and many a time in the early summer this deal was discussed among their friends. There was much shaking of heads and deep muttering against Jacob Paulsen. On the streets of Weeping Willow he boasted more loudly than ever of how he paid four cents more per bushel for Peter Grimsen's corn than the market price.

2

On the tenth day of July the whole family got into the spring wagon early in the forenoon for one of their Sunday visits to neighboring Danes. The old man, as the boys had come to call their father, even though he was only forty, drove the horses slowly for the first half-mile while passing his own fields. Never had Nebraska corn looked so well. Every row had already been laid by. It stood eight to ten feet tall, rich, green, beautifully waving in a gentle breeze that could hardly shake the dew-drenched stalks. Here and there, fine long tassels were already beginning to show their yellowish tops.

Peter felt for the first time as though he was on the way to victory. Today three thousand bushels seemed a very meagre estimate. He flexed his whip gently over the backs of his horses. "What do you think of that, Meta? Isn't that a fine field?"

"Yes, Peter, that is good." And she glanced at her four sons, two in the front seat with their father, two of them by her side. Neither she nor Peter wanted to talk. It was too pleasant on such a beautiful day to listen to the soft, sensuous rustle of the corn, feel the pleasant warmth of the morning sun, and let the thoughts of many things have their way. This was a good morning for Peter to pursue his endless calculations, and for Meta to plan for next winter and what she would have for the children and for the house. There were times now when she could even forget about Margaret for new life was stirring in her again. She expected another baby early in the fall. Perhaps it would be a girl.

3

At Peter Neilsen's there were four other Danish families, all farmers and all were in the gayest spirits. They talked of their crops and the prospects of corn prices should the yield be as great as it now seemed that it would be. Each boasted a little about his own particular prospects. Each one raised his expected yield per acre at least five bushels, and all of them talked of renting more land for the coming year. They also talked of Peter's loan and condemned Paulsen for the manner in which he had bound Peter to sell at a certain price, for they could afford to be free in their talk today. Twenty-five cents a bushel would be a good price for corn with the yield they would have this year. Anybody could see that. And so the talk ran on as they walked out through Nielsen's fields, examining the thick stalks, looking at yellow fields of wheat that would be ready for the binder in a day or two, wandering down into the pasture to see the cattle and finally back to the house for Mrs. Nielsen's fine Sunday dinner.

They were glad to get back to the house out of the sun, for the gentle breeze of the morning had turned into a warm southwest wind, and the thermometer had risen to ninety-six degrees by noon. There were sixteen of them at the first table and a whole flock of the younger kids who had to wait until their parents and the older children had eaten before they could be served. This was no great hardship for them since there would be greater freedom at the table if they could have it to themselves.

4

As soon as the dinner was over the boys began to organize for one of the principal games which they always played on these rare Sundays when they got together either at the Nielsen's or the Grimsen's. It was the Grimsen boys' own particular game and the others who happened to be present were compelled to submit to the superior leadership of those who had invented the game.

It had all come from reading a series of nickel novels published under the general title of *The James Boys*. These stories appeared as weekly publications and each paper-bound booklet contained a complete story of some wild and terrible exploit of the James Boys' gang in Missouri. Alfred Grimsen had gotten copies of these stories from a neighbor bachelor who had almost a complete collection of these tales. Alfred and David were the best authorities on these stories, but even Hans had begun to read them. But long before he could read David had told him many of the stories more than once. Hans knew the chief characters in this series as well as if he had read them all himself, and often when he was with the Nielsen boys he would retell for them the stories of murder, robbery and clever detective work that constituted the central theme in each individual story.

From these tales a game known as the James Boys had been developed. Each of the boys in the Grimsen and Nielsen family had a particular character which he impersonated, that is, all of them except Alfred, who usually considered himself too old for "such foolishness."

As soon as the dinner was over the whole gang gathered in an old stone quarry about a quarter of a mile from the house. Here the business of organization was settled. Since it always followed a fixed routine, not much time was wasted in getting ready for the game itself. First the assignments in the various parts of the drama were given out. Henry, the oldest of the Nielsen boys was to be Jesse James, and Hans was to play the part of Frank James. It was admitted that because Henry was the older he should be Jesse James, but it was also tactfully agreed that Frank James was the real brains of the James Boys' Gang.

Hans' brother David was the famous Carl Green, the detective, and Henry's brother Sigurd, and Hans' brother Frank were the leaders of the Younger Brothers, famous followers of Jesse James.

The first order of business was to cut long sticks to which were attached strings. These strings were the bridles, the sticks the horse. Next, Carl Green disappeared, and under the advice of Frank James and the leadership of Jesse the gang galloped off to a hiding place. It was an unwritten law that this hiding place should be so situated that Carl Green, the detective, could conceal himself near enough to overhear their sinister plans. Usually, their first plan would involve a raid upon the farm of Jacob Paulsen. This raid was inspired by a desire for moral justice, for these James' boys, like their prototypes in the nickel novels, never robbed or interfered with good people.

They were all gathered around their two chiefs, but before any definite plans could be made for the first great holdup of the day, there was another item of business to be settled. All of these boys chewed tobacco. Even Hans, since he was now eight years old and could be trusted not to tattle, had recently acquired the habit. It hadn't even made him sick, because David, profiting by the sad results of his first chew, had started Hans out very gradually with only a small "nip a day" for the first two weeks. As the James Boys' Gang they could not begin operations until each one had a chew tucked away in his cheek. After the first good spit, there was nothing that this "tough gang of robbers and highwaymen" would not undertake.

The problem of getting a sufficient supply of "regular," which was genuine chewing tobacco as opposed to such a poor substitute as cigar clippings, was not always easy to solve. A Sunday at the Nielsen's was nearly always a great success, however, from this point of view, because Henry Nielsen seemed never to fail them. He managed somehow to have a plug for these occasions.

As Jesse James and the leader of "the most bloodthirsty gang that ever robbed a bank" he drew a full plug from his hip pocket, took the first chew from the corner for himself, and then passed it around. His generosity was tempered with a reasonable threat as he said, "Now, damn you, take only a nip, or I'll not give you a second."

It went the rounds. At last it came to Hans, who was now, of course, called only Frank, and as Jesse's brother in crime deserved a little special attention, "Have a big one, Frank. This is going to be a dangerous business." Then, out of the corner of his mouth, with an intonation that everyone understood as indicating something outside the realm of reality, "I'll take it to David."

Then, while they all sat silent to indicate a complete absence of time and space, Jesse James gave Carl Green, the detective who lay in concealment behind a rock, a chew. Neither one spoke. It was almost as though they did not see each other.

This over, the real plotting began. Frank James speaking: "Cole Younger told me that Jacob Paulsen has just sold his corn, and that he took his money home. Let's go there first and string him up and take his cash. But you are not to hurt his wife." Then, for the benefit of Carl Green), "You know where his place is down behind the old hog house. After that we'll rob the bank in Weeping Willow—or what do you think, Jesse?"

"Yes, that will be all right. The Weeping Willow Bank is under the railroad bridge, and right up by the big oak tree near the swimming hole."

Then Cole Younger spoke up. "This is one time when we won't be bothered by Carl Green. I believe I got him the last time we held up the bank in Alvin."

"Yeah, you got him all right!" said Jim Younger, who today was played by Frank Grimsen. He was anxious to make a statement and spoke in a tense, earnest voice. He was new to these games, having only lately been considered old enough to be trusted with the secrets of the game, and with the fact that his brothers chewed tobacco. He was no longer a danger-ous tattle-tale.

The gang rode away to Jacob Paulsen's place. Here they worked unmolested, for it was understood that Carl Green would not come to the protection of this man. They charged around the hog house, and bat-tered down an imaginary door.

"Come out! Your days are numbered!" shouted Jesse.

Frank rushed through the door and in a moment came out dragging a piece of two-by-four.

"He begged like a dog for his life. Here, Jesse, is

the money. Now let's string him up." But first they
beat him, spat upon him, called him all the vile names
they knew so well.

"So you will cheat the farmers, will you?"

"You will drive poor men off their farms, will
you?"

And so on, till all had had a chance at the helpless
person of the hated Jacob Paulsen. Then they strung
him up to a projecting beam of the hog house, and all
fired their revolvers at him, revolvers that were cun-
ningly carved from pieces of wood.

Next came the raid on the Weeping Willow Bank.
But this proved a dismal failure, for no sooner had
they surrounded the bank than Carl Green began firing
at them from the upper branches of a tree where he
was completely concealed by the foliage. Cole Younger
was wounded and had to be held on his horse by one
of the boys. Frank James had his horse shot out from
under him, and for a moment he lay stunned on the
ground. Through a rain of bullets, Jesse turned back
and lifted his brother to the back of his saddle, and
they rode away. Around the corner and over the creek
to the swimming hole they rode. Here after account-
ing for their losses and dividing the money taken from
Jacob Paulsen they disbanded.

Carl, now as David, appeared. He was praised for
his clever work as a detective. They all claimed that
they had no idea he would have concealed himself in
that tree. After a little more discussion they began to
strip for swimming.

The swimming hole was at a bend in the creek where the current during flood seasons had hollowed out a depression that even in the summer time, when the stream was very low, measured a depth of twelve feet near the farther bank. Here the boys could dive either from the bank itself or from the branches of an overhanging tree. On the side of the stream where they entered the water was a sloping bank about thirty feet in length. On this incline they made a grooved slippery-slide by throwing water with their hands from the creek, or carrying it up in their hats.

The swimming was in full swing: some diving, some water-fighting, others plastering themselves with mud from the creek, and still others diving from the tree. All at once Hans spied a little black dog with white spots on its breast, walking along the bank and looking as if it wished to play.

"Whose dog is that?" said Hans.

"Oh, that's Pete's dog. You know, the man who caught us in his watermelon patch last year," said Sigurd. "He's a . . ., too."

No one knew whether he meant the man or the dog, or to whom the "too" referred, nor did they care. The dog's name was Shep. It was not long until Shep was swimming in the water with the boys. Finally someone said, "Why don't we see how long he can keep afloat in the water?"

This was a real challenge. Someone caught him by the tail and held him in the deep water.

Now began a long, tedious and violent form of tor-

ture. The boys gathered on the bank to watch the fun
and to take turns holding the dog's tail. Fifteen minutes, half an hour, and an hour went by. The torture
had now fanned the spirit of the group into a bloodthirsty mob. Sigurd finally said, "We can't drown him
that way. I'll hold him under the water."

In the meantime the little dog barked occasionally.
It was a weak, pitiful, little bark, asking as near as a
dog can ask for sympathy, for help. Hans cheered with
the others for the dog's destruction. He had been sorry
for it at first, but now he was as violent as all the others
in demanding that the dog be killed. Soon the attempt
at drowning the dog wore out Sigurd's patience. He
swung the dog over his head, still holding it by the
tail, and then threw it up on the bank. Here it lay,
sick and panting for breath. In anger, or pity, or unreasoning fury, no one, not even himself could tell which,
Hans grasped a heavy club and beat out the dog's
brains, hammering it until its head was a mashed pulp
on the bank of the stream. All of the boys watched
without a word. A quiet had fallen on the group. No
one talked. It was as though each one in turn waited for
the other to speak, waited angrily, accusingly, futilely.

Finally David said, "I'm thirsty. Let's get to hell
out of here."

Each one ran for the water to wash off the mud and
then dress in furious haste. Sigurd was the first to
get dressed. Up the bank and away he went. Others
followed in rapid succession. Suddenly, there was an
awful wailing as though someone had suffered a ter-

rible injury. Looking around, David saw his little brother Hans struggle nervously with his shirt, which in his haste he had pulled on back to front.

"Don't leave me! Don't leave me! Wait for me!" he cried. David rushed over to help him, and then he suddenly realized that he was frightened. Back in the tall weeds and underbrush an ominous silence had taken upon itself a physical power that clutched at the heart and caused a reeling, dizzy sensation in the brain. All the boys were gone now, gone like a flash up on the bank and out of sight.

David grabbed Hans' pants in one hand, and leading him with the other, he rushed him screaming with fear up the bank and after the other boys. In a minute they reached an open space in the woods near the railroad track. Here, at a short distance the other boys were waiting. David now stopped and helped Hans into his clothes.

"What were you screaming for anyway? Are you a damn baby to be afraid?"

So David talked to cover his own fear. Everybody knew the truth, but no more was said to David and Hans. Henry gave David the first nip as he passed chewing again. Thus fortified, they left the dead dog with its battered and bleeding head hammered into the mud. They left him there, but for Hans, and perhaps for some of the others, it was not possible to leave behind the memory of the dog's pleading eyes, his soft little body, his faint pitiful bark. These qualities detached themselves from the dead thing in the mud and came along. They came through the open spot in the wood, across the railroad tracks and over the dusty road home that afternoon. In days to come these memories followed close as the boys walked by the old, dark hole near their home at night. Up the stairs they came to the little bedroom, and then, on through the years they followed roads that were long and crooked, but they followed. Perhaps they would sometimes get lost for a month, a year, but sooner or later they would catch up again, following, softly, unobtrusively: the gentle eyes, the soft body, the faint, pitiful, little bark.

5

In their playing and swimming they had not noticed how the soft warmth of the day had changed to a dry stifling heat. It was not till they began walking back to the house for afternoon coffee that they felt the burning sting of the hot winds from the southwest. The ties on the railroad track which they followed were so warm they burned the feet and no one would take a dare to step on the rails for an instant.

When they reached the house they found the men already at the coffee table, although it was only a little past three o'clock. The vigorous joy of the morning's conversation was gone. There was some attempt at talking, but it was of that forced type which takes the form of questions and answers. For the past hour the men had stood by the north side of the house watching the hot winds begin to shrivel the corn. They had heard of hot winds from the southwest that could dry up the corn, but none of them had been in Nebraska long enough to really experience them. This afternoon they burned so hot that it did not seem as though a man could endure facing them for any length of time.

They began talking about going home even before coffee time, but Hans Nielsen would not tolerate such a suggestion, nor did they really mean to do anything as unheard of as that. Mrs. Nielsen had hurried up the preparation of the coffee, and now they sat around the table trying to keep the talk going, but each one busy with thoughts of his corn fields and of his live stock.

They began to rise from the table. "Now, don't be in a hurry to get home. You can't stop the wind by being at home any more than you can by staying here," said Nielsen. "It's a long time till darkness comes these days."

"Yes, that's true enough," said one, "but I must do my chores before dark, you know."

"I am not sure that my cattle have enough water," said another.

No one told the real reason why he was hurrying away at least two hours earlier than the customary time for departure. No one exactly admitted the truth to himself. The truth that lurked in their thoughts was too terrible to believe. Somehow or other it was as though admission of the truth might have some effect in bringing it to pass. As a frightened animal in danger seeks its lair, or as a horse driven from a burning barn will rush back into the flames to certain death, so the farmer, when his crops are in danger, hurries home as though he believed that his presence there could still the floods or stop the wind.

Four o'clock came, and the hot winds which usually die down by three-thirty were still blowing. Each half hour seemed to tell on the fields. In Peter Grimsen's wagon there was no sound except the occasional complaints of the children as they hid their faces behind straw hats used as shields against the wind. The horses labored without sweating in the day's terrific heat. The temperature at Nielsen's at three o'clock had been one hundred and nine degrees in the shade.

Now they topped the hill and could see their own corn fields. Till this moment, they had hoped without reason that their fields would not look like all the others they had passed. As a man will search over and over in his pockets for an object he has lost, when he knows it cannot possibly be there, so they had hoped for the hopeless. The truth was only too clear. Where the waving, green corn had covered the gentle slopes that morning, they saw shriveled stalks. It seemed as though the leaves had not only fallen to the sides of the stalks, but that the stalks had actually shrunk about two feet in size. Everywhere the bare ground was visible in the fields.

The dogs lay in the shade of the house and did not even come to welcome the family home. The cattle stood under the ragged willows by the barn. They were all facing the north, and they hung their heads low as in despair. It was still only five in the afternoon, yet the chickens had gone to roost. There was no sign of welcome—only the steady, even push of the south-west wind. It was not a strong wind. It rustled the now dried leaves of the cottonwoods with a sinister, persistent, rattling noise. The sun hung red, large and hot in the West. A stillness, made awful by some regular, maddening noise, like the drip of a faucet in the middle of the night, pervaded the atmosphere.

Peter Grimsen did not sleep that night. Before dawn he was walking slowly along the rows of his best field of corn. He often stooped to feel of the dried leaves, but without hope, for the usual healing dews of Nebraska had not come that night to the parched and thirsting corn. Peter walked through the rows, stopping to feel of the stalks, to draw the dry blades through his hands.

"If the wind is now over, it will recover," he said to himself. "There is still moisture enough in the ground to carry it on till the next rain comes."

That night the farmers in Weeping Willow heard that the hot winds were blowing over the whole corn belt. The talk went that the second day had been as bad as the first, and that it was doubtful now if corn would make twenty bushels to the acre. There was also talk of a rise in the market prices.

The third day was the worst of all. Peter Grimsen's hills looked positively bare. It was as though no corn had been planted at all. The crop was completely gone, or so it seemed. Perhaps there would not even be feed enough in the stalks for the cattle next winter.

"Now we have reached the end, Meta. I don't see how I can go on longer. Three years in Massachusetts and now three here. We came to this country with over four thousand kroner, and now we are in debt to everyone we meet. I can't go to town without having someone ask me for money I haven't got. The children are in rags. What will the winter be like?"

"I don't know, Peter. Many times I think of going home to the old country, but how would that help, to come there with empty hands? And how would we get there? Where would we get the money for tickets for all our children and ourselves? There is nothing we can do. Oh, if we had only stayed in Denmark!"

For a moment Peter thought she would burst into tears. He felt bitterly the cut of the last remark. He knew that her thoughts had gone back to Margaret. For though neither had ever spoken of it, they both knew that in Denmark their child would not have died of whooping-cough. At last Meta spoke again.

"But I am glad we are here in America. Our children will not have to be farmers. They can rise to better things in this democratic country."

"Then let us go to bed," said Peter. These good words that had cost her so much, were words of peace and courage.

The winds ceased on the fourth day, and gradually the corn began to recover. It was like magic to see the power for recovery the corn still possessed. Late July brought rains and there was promise of a small crop. In the meantime the general failure of crops

throughout the corn belt was marked by a steady rise
in prices.

6

The last months of this weary summer were doubly
difficult for Meta. When Margaret had been born, she
had hoped that she would not have more children.
Four sons and a daughter seemed like an ideal family.
But things happened that one could not foresee nor
understand, and now she was expecting a baby again.
Perhaps it would be a girl, and then everything would
come right for them once more. "There must be some
meaning to all this struggle," she thought. "How can
there help being a meaning?" she added, as if to stifle
the rising words of doubt.

Her child was born in September, and it was another
son. People were very kind. It was not a busy time of
the year, and during her week in bed she had visitors
on three separate days. The women folks brought her
gifts for the child. The prettiest thing she had ever
owned in America was given her by Mrs. Hansen, the
groceryman's wife, although she herself did not come
to visit Meta. It was a little baby's quilt and it was
made of real silk. It was the sort of thing one could
have used for a baby girl. Meta put it away after the
week of visiting was over. Peter asked about it once,
but got no answer. It was never used for the new baby
nor did anyone ever see it again, except Meta.

That fall when Alfred and David quit school to help

with the corn-shucking, Peter ordered Hans to stay out also. "You can help a little by watching the cattle in the corn-stalks, but mostly you can stay in the house and help your mother."

"Oh, maybe I don't need to have him do that," said Meta.

"Yes, that is the way I want it arranged," he replied.

"Then, I say, thank you," Meta answered.

The corn-shucking came to an end, and Peter Grimsen had sixteen hundred bushels of corn in his cribs. His yield had averaged twenty bushels to the acre, and the stalks were good enough to provide adequate feeding for his cattle. It was remarkable the ways things could happen, the way this country could save them from complete destruction, reduce them to despair and then revive their hopes again. The land had not failed them after all, but they still had Jacob Paulsen to consider.

When Peter shelled his corn, he delivered twelve hundred bushels to Paulsen's account in the elevator. The day it was delivered corn was sixty-one cents a bushel in Weeping Willow. On his three-hundred-dollar loan Paulsen had made a profit of four hundred and thirty-two dollars. Peter, inspired by the sore need of his family, humbled himself to Paulsen, and asked him to share the profit fifty-fifty. He should have spared himself that humiliation, for Paulsen only cursed him and accused him of trying to break his word.

"I bought the corn and gave you the money when you needed it. I took a big risk. I helped you when no one else would, and now you ask me to divide with you. No, by God, I bought that corn and paid for it, and I am going to keep it, you can be damn sure of that."

Peter saw the futility of reply, but he answered, "The day may come, Jacob Paulsen, when the world will know you for the dirty dog you are."

VII

"IF YOU ever see one of them Grimsen boys, you better look around a bit, there'll be two more of them right near." Thus old man Day expressed himself, and he believed that he ought to know. More than once he had caught them in his apple orchard or strawberry patch. Other people knew that Day was speaking the truth. If you saw one of them on the top of the threshing machine when it was quiet at the noon hour, it might be well to glance around, for another one might be taking a little peek into the general storage box under the machine, where the Benson boys kept their chewing tobacco.

David, Hans, and Frank had made a few contacts with other boys, but none that meant much to them compared with the loyalty they felt toward each other. They read, played, and worked together. It was mostly work, though, on Grimsen's farm. At five o'clock every morning they were doing the chores. At sundown they came home from the fields tired, but still ready for such adventure as the night might hold in store for them. Even their father discovered that he could not separate them in the fields. Once he sent David to cultivate in one field and ordered Hans and Frank to cut milkweeds in a patch at the opposite side of the farm. Late in the afternoon he had gone over to the fields in order to see how they had progressed with their work to find that not a single weed had been cut, nor could he find the boys anywhere. He hurried back home in a rage, believing that the boys had played hookey and gone swimming, or "some such-like foolishness," as he always called it.

When he got home Meta could give him no information. Just as he was beginning to lecture Meta on the many faults of his children, he saw the three boys coming in from the field together. David was riding one horse, Hans and Frank were on the other. Long before they reached the house he could hear them laughing and talking.

"Take it easy, Peter," said Meta.

"I thought I told you kids to cut milkweeds over on the hill by the horse pasture."

"Yes," said Hans, "but there were so many more milkweeds where David was cultivating, that we thought it would be best to go there first."

"We can finish that patch tomorrow," said Frank, a little worried, since it looked for a moment as though there would be a scene.

Peter smiled in spite of himself. Here was his nine-year-old son planning the work on the farm, and refusing to take orders. "Well, well, Hans, so that's the way you have figured it out is it? All right. You and Frank work it out your own way, but be sure of one thing, I want all those weeds cut by the time we are through with the cultivating."

"Ah, they can easy do that," said David, and there

the argument ended, nor did Peter again try to separate them in the fields. He couldn't even send one of them to town alone, for no matter how he planned it they would defeat him either by their own devices or with the help of Meta, so that when the actual time came for going to town there would be at least two of them on the wagon seat, and usually all three.

There was only one time of the year when they had to work alone and that was during shucking time. They recognized the necessity of that and did not object. Even then when Hans was watching the cattle, which had become his particular task, he would often sneak away to ride on the turn with David and follow him down the row as long as he dared to be away from the cattle.

Usually such visits were prompted by necessity as well as pleasure, for since Hans was the youngest of the boys who chewed tobacco, he was often in woeful need. David and Alfred were usually pretty well supplied, because they could add an order for an extra plug or two on the grocery list, and then slip it out of the box before the groceries were carried into the house. Since neither of their parents read English nor checked the list very closely this trick had worked very well. Hans was at the mercy of his older brothers, and they dealt fairly with him, but even so, he was often caught short. Since he had become chief cattle herder, he felt that the world owed him "chewin'," or that somebody did.

2

Fall had come again. For two hours Hans had been following the cattle back and forth along the corn rows, and it was still only ten o'clock. Four hours every forenoon and three hours every afternoon it was his task to watch the cattle in the newly shucked field. Tobacco was such a comfort to him at this task which required no constructive labor. It helped to pass the slow moving hours. It was only the middle of the forenoon, as one could easily tell by facing the north and observing the direction of one's shadow. He did not have even a nip of "chewin'," and he knew that it would not do to ask his brothers. They had been on limited rations for the past two days. No one had been to town for groceries for two weeks, and all of the old man's plugs of Horse Shoe had been sliced once already. It was a fixed law that no one should slice them a second time. Their father was not a keen observer, but even so, he would no doubt find them out if they carried a good thing too far. "If he ever finds out what we are doing there will be Hell to pay," said David. Hans remembered this warning. He ought to remember it. "Don't they tell me often enough," he muttered, for as the craving grew stronger, he could not help feeling a little resentment toward his brothers and their undisputed prior rights. Why should he be compelled to suffer, and anyway, how could they be so sure that the old man would discover that his plugs were being sliced if Hans broke the rule just once.

Thus by a series of questions he weakened the voice of his conscience, until it became quite clear that the thing for him to do was to invent some means by which he might get home, and elude his mother long enough to cut himself a slice of chewing tobacco. The more he worked on the specific details of his plans, the more insignificant the moral issue became. It was not long until it seemed as though the moral issue demanded that he be supplied with "chewin'."

Circumstances were apparently in his favor, for before he could decide just what to do, the cows, always under the leadership of Old Red, the Three Teat, had turned around and were feeding slowly in the direction of the house. This was the exact opposite direction to the unshucked corn which it was his task to protect. The only question was, could he now trust them to go down this particular section long enough for him to reach the house?

"But I must have a chew," he said, and talking aloud to himself as was his practice, "A fellow can't go here day after day without chewin' tobacco. I don't mind not having regular all the time, but by God, I won't go a whole day without something to chew. It ain't right anyway. Damn if it is. I'll just run over by the fir trees and crawl in the back door. Mother will be in the kitchen and I'll cut a slice even if it's been cut before."

This plan of entering by the "back" door seemed very reasonable, for although it was the parlor door, and really the front door, in Peter Grimsen's house it was always called the back door. The kitchen door was known as the front door because it led to and from the realm that ruled their lives.

He took one last look at the cows and ran for the house. It was at least forty rods' distance, and when he reached the back door, just ready to enter, his mother came around the corner of the house with a few pieces of washing to hang on the line, mostly diapers.

"Why, son, what are you doing here?"

"Oh, I was hungry, and the cattle are all right for a little while, so I thought I could have a piece of bread." Thank goodness he was prepared with an answer should he be caught.

"Yes, but why did you come around this way? Aren't the cattle over on the three-cornered piece?"

"Well, you know, I lost my knife yesterday, and I thought I might have lost it here." ·

"All right, come into the kitchen."

There in the comfort of the kitchen, he sat at the table while his mother gave him a large piece of bread with apple butter and a cup of coffee. As he ate his bread and drank his coffee, he realized that what he had told his mother was mostly the truth—or so it seemed to him, for he was really hungry. But how was he to get into the parlor to slice the old man's plug? If he could stay here long enough, he knew it could be done, but time was pressing. How long would the cattle stay out of the unhusked corn?

"Mother, why don't you hang up those clothes?"

"Oh, there's no hurry about that," and she continued with her work at the stove. "But you better hurry, for you know what will happen to you if your father sees the cows in the corn field."

Yes, he knew well enough, but couldn't he get his mother out of the room, even for a little while? He looked at the water bucket, and saw that the dipper was down to the bottom.

"Mother, can I have a cup of water?"

"Do you want water with your coffee? That's the craziest thing I've heard yet."

"But I'm really thirsty."

She went to the pail, and finding it empty, she picked it up and walked out the door. Now was his chance. Like a flash, and silent as a cat he made for the parlor door. As he placed his hand on the knob, his mother's voice called from the outside: "Hans, Hans, hurry! The cows are out on the road!"

"Oh, hell, and God damn!" he muttered under his breath. When he reached the front door he saw them over half a mile off, walking steadily, and as he suspected, with Old Red in the lead. He began to run, for he knew by bitter experience that they would get at least one mile away before he caught them. He cut across the fields, heading for the corner, a mile off, hoping by the short cut to reach it before the cattle. Tired and out of breath, and almost sick with running, he climbed through the hedge at the corner and looked up the road expecting to see the cattle. But they were nowhere in sight. He walked to the cross roads and looked in every direction, but no cattle were there.

"How can this be, I wonder? They must have stopped when she got them out on the road."

He walked to the top of the hill, and there, a quarter of a mile down the road, he saw his cattle, stopped, and he saw why. A boy was standing there with a stick in his hand.

Hans knew who it was before he got to him. He knew it was the widower Albert Polk's boy, who had recently come to live with his father.

"Hallo," offered Hans as he came up.

"Hello. Are these your cattle?"

"Sure. I'm glad you stopped them. Are you Mr. Polk's boy?"

"Yeah. What's your name?"

"Hans Grimsen."

"My name's Herman Polk."

The cattle were now feeding by the side of the road, so the boys sat down. Hans looked closely at Herman thinking, "I wonder if he chews?" The more he studied him, the more certain he became that he did, for it looked as though there might be a stain of tobacco in the corner of his mouth. But how to approach the subject, that was the problem.

"You goin' to be here long?" said Hans.

"Guess so. Dad says he's goin' to keep me to do his cookin'."

"Then you'll go to school here after corn shucking."

"Yeah. Got many kids there?"

"Bout thirty," said Hans, and then seeing the proper opening, "And most of the boys chew tobacco, too."

Herman put both hands in his pockets and was silent as though he were thinking about this. Finally he said, "You don't chew, I guess?"

"Well, once in a while I do. I guess you ain't got none now, have you?"

Herman looked up quickly. "No, but maybe we could get some."

"Could we? How?"

"I always cut my old man's plugs. . . ."

"Do you? So do I," interrupted Hans, as joy surged in his heart, for he knew he had found a real friend. There was something about Herman that was different. Somehow he did not act like the other boys at the school. He was straightforward. He was real.

"When can we, Herman?"

"Well, this morning I acted like I was asleep when Dad got up, 'cause I figured he'd be changing the hiding place of his tobacco. He always does; about once a week. I saw him take it out of his felt boot, and leave the house with it."

"Do you always try to watch?"

"No, I just watch for fun, 'cause I can always find it. There was only once when I didn't find it, and that time he had forgotten to hide it, and it lay right on the kitchen table, among the dishes. If I had washed the dishes as I was s'posed to I'd a seen it."

"Where do you think it is now?"

"I don't know, I was just startin' to look for it when your cattle came up the road. But it's down around the barn somewhere. Let's go see."

"All right. I'll just throw a rock at that Old Red. She's a bastard. You know what we did? Last night David and I took her to the bull up at Square's place, and he served her seven times."

"Seven times! God a'mighty, that's a lot."

"It sure is," said Hans.

They reached the barn. Inside the door they stopped to inspect the place. Both were experienced in the art of searching for hidden tobacco. Almost instantly they sensed that each followed the same procedure. They studied the whole lay-out with the eyes of experienced detectives. They would have been ashamed to indulge in random hunting. Two places were investigated without result. The third was the granary. One glance revealed a depression in the loose shelled corn about four feet from the door. And there, after one thrust of the hand the tobacco was found. Herman brought a butcher knife from the kitchen. There were five plugs, and each was carefully sliced. After each slice was cut off the plug was rubbed against the wall very gently to remove the trace of the fresh edge of the plug.

With five long slices in his hand, Herman led the way back to the road. He now divided one slice into two pieces, and each put his share in his mouth. Herman then gave Hans two slices and kept two for himself. This was one of the most generous acts that Hans had ever seen. It meant a pledge of friendship for life.

Together they drove the cattle back into the field. The rest of the morning passed quickly. Hans invited Herman to dinner, which he accepted providing his

father would permit him. Thus began a long series of
visits back and forth that lasted through corn-husking
time, and into the school days that followed.

3

The easy days of midwinter gave Peter more time in
the house than he seemed ever to have had before. The
boys did most of the chores, and there was not much
trouble in caring for the stock, since there were warm
sheds for all the animals. It was easy to see, though,
that Peter was planning something else. Meta guessed
what it was and that he had not yet made up his mind
to speak out about it.

What kept Peter silent was that he did not especially
like to hear Meta's opinion on the subject that was
uppermost in his mind, probably because subcon-
sciously he believed that she was right. At last one day
it came out of him. "Meta, I believe I'll have to go to
town for a load of lumber."

"Lumber?" said Meta in a questioning tone. "You
are not planning to build an extra room to the house
are you?"

"Now, Meta, don't be foolish. I have decided that
with all those brood sows I have this year, that I'll
need more space in my hog house. What's the use of
having brood sows, if they have to lie on the top of
each other and crush their pigs to death as soon as they
are born?"

"Perhaps not, but what's the use of spending and

spending on this place. Why, you act as if you owned it, but some day the landlord will come and ask you to move. You'll see he'll take it all away from us. Why can't you get along with what you have, or at least get him to pay for part of it?"

That was a long speech from Meta, and Peter listened in silence. She was afraid she had said too much for he might fly into one of his towering rages. Strangely enough he merely sat in silence for a time and then went out to do a little work around the barn.

It was not long before he was to discover how right Meta had been. A week or so later Jacob Paulsen came driving into the yard. He was all smiles when he came to the kitchen. Meta greeted him with a sinking feeling, because she knew that after what Peter had told him the year of the loan on his crop, Jacob bore them no good will.

"Good day, Mr. Paulsen. Will you come in?"

"Oh, no, I guess not. Is your man at home?"

"Yes. He's down by the barn."

"Well, I'll go see him. You have nice outbuildings here, don't you? I suppose Mr. Hobson bought the lumber for them."

"No. We bought it ourselves."

"You did! Well, well, that will be quite a loss to you when you move away, won't it?" Then with his thumbs in his vest armholes, "But that's the way it is when you are mere renters. Hum. Three corn-cribs. You have good crops here. Well, well, I must see your man. Good-bye."

Meta closed the door almost before he had turned his back.

"Now there will be trouble, I can see that. The fat swine." And she turned to her stove.

Before long, she watched him drive away. She had the coffee-pot on the fire, for she believed Peter would soon be in, and she also believed that he would not bring Paulsen with him. If a Dane called on another and was not invited to coffee, it was considered a direct insult, but it was the common talk around Weeping Willow that no one, not even the renters on his own farms, ever invited Jacob Paulsen to coffee.

Peter came and rather solemnly sat down at the table. Meta poured his coffee, and then he spoke.

"You saw Jacob was here, didn't you?"

"Yes. What did he want?"

"I am not quite sure, but I know he did not come to do me any good. He talked of all our improvements on the place. He congratulated me on having such a good place for the low rent I am paying. That was about all. This is the last year of our lease, and for a long time I have been thinking of going to see Mr. Hobson about re-renting the place."

"You should have done that before. Why don't you go today?"

"Oh, there's no hurry about it."

"Yes, there is. I wish you would have the boys hitch up the team, so that you could go over there now."

For a long time he sat quietly. The only sound in the kitchen was the ringing of his coffee cup as he drew its bottom with a deft movement across the saucer after each time he poured out the coffee from his cup. The cup was now empty, but he still drew it over the saucer as if punctuating his thoughts. "All right, I'll do it," he said.

When he arrived at Mr. Hobson's place, he could easily see that something was wrong.

"I don't know, Mr. Grimsen, whether I want to rent the place again. I have sort of thought of starting one of my own boys farming over there. But I don't know."

"If that's what you want to do, why haven't you told me? You should have let me know that before this time, if I am to rent another place. You know I have farmed it now for three years, and farmed it well."

"Yes, I know that, but I believe it's worth more than you pay. I could get more for it now."

"Yes, now, after I have fenced it and built new cribs and outhouses. Maybe you could, but don't I get any credit for that?"

"I didn't ask you to do that, did I? It's none of my business that you spent your money on my farm."

"No, but it would be justice if you gave me some credit for it. Now that I have made it a good rent farm, am I to leave it?"

"No. No. You can have it, but you see, I have been offered seven hundred dollars a year rent for it, which is two hundred and twenty more than you pay, so I don't see how I can refuse that. Now if you want it at that price, you can have it."

"Who offered you that? Was it Jacob Paulsen?"

"Yes, if you want to know, it was."

"So that was it. That's how he is trying to push me off. You know, Mr. Hobson, he has done that to other rent farmers in order to boost his own rents. He doesn't want that farm and you know it. Why not be honest with me?"

"He does want it. See this check for one hundred dollars? He gave me that as earnest money yesterday. I was planning to go to see you today."

"Well, I won't get off. And I won't pay the extra rent this year. And you can't put me off because you haven't notified me soon enough. The law will be on my side."

"We'll see about that, Mr. Grimsen."

"Yes, we will, Mr. Hobson. Good day."

Peter Grimsen didn't know much about law, but his sense of justice told him that he was in the right this time. On his way home he drove by Weeping Willow, and went directly to a lawyer. This was the first time he had ever had occasion to see a member of the legal profession, but he assumed that the lawyers were a class of people who were interested in justice. Peter Grimsen did not know that law and justice are not synonymous terms. However, in this case the law was on the side of justice, so the lawyer told Mr. Grimsen. He advised Peter to "sit tight" and that if they started legal action against him he could win his case easily. The lawyer told him that the legal time for notice to move had passed and that he could stay another year at the same rent he had paid during the past three years.

With this consolation, he returned home. At least he would have one year in which to plan for another place. But his peace of mind was soon destroyed on that point. Three days later the lawyer appeared at the farm. He made a long and detailed explanation, most of which was so filled with legal terms that Peter could not even understand half of what he said. The point was, as the lawyer explained, that since Mr. Grimsen had a written lease in which a definite date of expiration was fixed, a notice to move off was not required by law, as would have been the case had the agreement been verbal.

"It's true, they can't put you off the place without going to court, but they can demand a reasonable raise in the rent."

The lawyer now produced a new lease, and before it was all over, Mr. Grimsen had signed the new lease for seven hundred and twenty dollars rent a year. This lease was to expire at the end of four years.

It was not until over a year later that he learned what had really happened. Mr. Hobson had told Paulsen about Peter's visit, and they surmised that he would go to the lawyer in Weeping Willow. Acting upon that prediction, they had gone to the lawyer, and after paying him twenty-five dollars, they got him to change his story and force a new lease upon Peter Grimsen. The lawyer charged Mr. Grimsen only ten dollars for the legal services he had rendered him.

VIII

AFTER CHRISTMAS the Grimsen boys were again back at school. During the winter and up till the beginning of spring work on the farm there were about forty children at the Laurel Hope School. It was located at a cross roads on a piece of land about one hundred yards square. The yard was surrounded by thorn trees and a heavy growth of weeds crowded the playground up to the door of the school house. No farmer ever took the time to run a mower over the playground, but in time the weeds would be trampled down and a space cleared for ball games in the fall and for fox and geese after the snow had come.

The Grimsen boys had remained antagonistic to the children at the school since that bitter reception on the first day three years before. They had taken part in the games, adjusting themselves to the life of the school, but in all those three years they had made no close friends among the boys they had met there. They had never been invited to the homes of the children at the school, nor on their part had they made any effort to become very intimate with their playmates. The Grimsen boys resented the treatment given them that first year too deeply even to care for any closer contacts than those necessary to carry on the ordinary games during recesses and at noons. As soon as school was over the four brothers, Frank was also in school this winter, were the first to leave the building. There were other boys who went their way, but the Grimsen boys never waited for them. They walked by themselves, glad to be alone after a day with these American children, whose way of life still seemed strange to these Danish boys.

This particular winter had been unusually turbulent. The teacher was a self-complacent, little woman about twenty-five years old. She was short, stocky, well dressed, and to some people of her own age she may even have appeared beautiful. She ruled by means of terror rather than love. Nothing disturbed a sort of hard, superior smile that seemed to be frozen on her face. The smile implied that she was master, and that all was well with her. She came from Weeping Willow, where she was one of the leaders in the social life of the Methodist Church. Her name was Mildred Crow. Every suggestion that there might be evil in the world was countered by denial, and that hard, frozen smile.

If the pupils ever indicated that there might be something bad about the loss of life in the Civil War, her reply was, "It's all good. God in His wisdom knows best." Then that smile. Her religion seemed to fit her well for her task as she conceived it, for since she did not believe in the reality of evil, it served as a good excuse for the expression of her natural sadistic impulses.

One of her favorite pastimes was to stand at the back

of the room with eyes roving and lips slightly moist as if that frozen smile chilled them, watching the children as a man with a fly swatter watches for flies to kill, especially after they have annoyed him a great deal. If she spied the slightest infraction of rules, she would silently approach the pupil from the rear and hit him across the fingers with a short, heavy stick, which she always carried as the symbol of her power. She never told the pupil what his offense had been, nor did she warn him of her intentions. Many times, before the pupils understood her tactics, a boy, noticing her approach and seeing her smile, would smile back at her, expecting some kind word. Cruelly, and not undeceiving him, she would walk up to his desk and then hit him across the back of his hands. Her blows were sometimes severe enough to cause pain that would last for several days. It was the firm belief of the boys that she punished them even when they did not deserve it.

From the first day Hans had gone to school, he had learned not to expect kindness, fairness, or anything that could be called by the name of decency at the Laurel Hope School. But he had, at least once, had a teacher who was kindhearted and friendly. The one who preceded Mildred Crow was Danish. She was plump, attractive, laughter-loving, and kind. Her rule at Laurel Hope had been characterized by remarkable success, for what others had failed to accomplish by cruelty, she achieved by being honest, and just. She made a deep impression on Hans and helped him more than any other teacher he ever had at Laurel Hope. He had clashed with her on only one issue. That was the study of Grammar. He had failed to comprehend the significance of Grammar, and decided that it was one subject he would never study. Miss Jorgensen had tried to persuade him, but all to no avail. One night she kept him after school and talked it over with him. She tried various arguments. Finally she said, "Don't you like the way I teach it? Are you doing this because you don't like me?"

This cut him deeply, for she was the only teacher he had ever cared for.

"Oh, no, Miss Jorgensen. No. I like you best of all. But I hate Grammar."

"Why do you hate it?"

"I don't know, but I hate it, and I won't study it. Never, never."

He won his battle then, and also later with Miss Crow. She had tried punishing him by hitting his hands with her stick, but it was soon clear, even to her, that Hans would not study Grammar. Another thing was soon apparent to her also, and that was that Hans read his lessons so well that he could catch her in mistakes. He never failed to mention these mistakes before the class. This humiliated her and gave the whole class secret pleasure. They warned Hans, and at the same time egged him on. Eventually this led to disaster for Hans, but not exactly because he questioned the teacher's knowledge.

There was in the school a girl named Ethel Square.

Hans and his brothers knew her well, both in school
and out, for it was her father who always kept a bull
for breeding purposes. Grimsen's boys had led their
cows to Square's place many times to get them bred.
One night they had seen Ethel hiding in the bushes by
the barn yard watching the show. This had given rise
to much rather indelicate talk. Whenever any of the
boys wanted to tease their brother David, they would
shout, "David loves Ethel. David loves Ethel." And
often less delicate suggestions would be made. This
spread to the school until Ethel and David became
mortal enemies. She, in her dull, oxlike manner would
attack him unawares with a sort of emotionless, prosaic
viciousness. One day, when he was sitting on the school
porch, she walked calmly past and without a word, or
even a suggestion of passion, she hit him over the head
with a baseball bat.

Hans hated her as much as did his brothers. One day
in reading class it fell to her lot to read a certain section
of *The Wreck of the Hesperus*. When she came to the
verse: "The sea roared like an angry bull," she read,
"the sea roared. . . . The sea roared like. . . . The sea
roared like. . . ."

Hans could stand this no longer. This was an insult
to a great poem, an insult to literature.

"Say Bull, say it," he almost screamed.

Miss Crow lost her Christian smile for the first time
in her career at Laurel Hope. Hans had violated her
most cherished faith in the asexual purity of all things
by emphasizing the reality of bulls. To her, no doubt,

a bull was not only vulgar, but one of the many evils the reality of which should be denied.

"Hans, leave the class and go to your seat. Leave now." Her voice rose almost to a scream. Ethel was crying, the whole school was tense, electrified.

"And, Hans, stay after school. Do you hear? Do you?" Again her voice rose to a scream.

But Hans did not answer. He had returned to his seat where he sat as nearly unconcerned in outward appearance as was possible, looking out of the window. Under his breath he was trying to relieve his emotions. "God damn her soul to hell forever." This phrase he repeated slowly, carefully, and steadily. It made him feel better. He knew that he was in the right.

All morning he sat in his seat, nursing his grievance, at times almost in tears. The one class that he enjoyed most of all was the reading class, and of all the poems in the book, *The Wreck of the Hesperus* was his favorite. He had memorized the whole poem, and that very morning he had planned to recite without the book when the teacher asked him to read. Ethel had spoiled that, but his hatred did not vent itself on her, for he realized that she was an ox, but it burned with a steady, revengeful fire against Miss Crow. Now she was smiling again. Damn her soul to hell forever!

The noon hour was full of plotting among the boys on the play-ground. Everyone sympathized with Hans. They advised him to run away, to go home, to tell his father. All this he knew was futile. How could he tell his father? His father didn't read English and would not appreciate the poem anyway. He would think his son had been disobedient and would probably give him a whipping and send him back. The only thing he could do was to stay and take it at school.

When school was over, Miss Crow left Hans in his seat, while she swept out the room. Her smile was even broader than usual as she went about her work. Hans sat still and tense, tense with an anger that dulled the edge of fear. He stared straight before him at the eternal mottoes in red and green chalk on the blackboard, copied from *Progressive Course in English*, by E. J. Hoenshel. This book that he hated so, and which he refused to study was the source for the expressions that never failed to appear on the blackboard. They were changed at irregular intervals. The present mottoes had been there for a month—two of them:

Golden palaces break men's rest, and purple robes cause restless nights.

It is the finest thing in the world to live: most people only exist.

When the teacher had finished sweeping the room, she turned to Hans. "Hans, go out and cut two switches, and bring them to me."

"So I am to cut my own switches, am I?" he said to himself, as he walked to the road where there was a box elder tree with long, slender shoots. "I'll cut them long. Then she'll not be able to swing them very hard," thought Hans. He picked two about six feet long and brought them to the teacher.

"Take your seat again."

It was like being in a death cell. "Why can't she get it over with? If this keeps up much longer we'll have to explain why we are late at home," he thought. Now she was erasing the mottoes on the blackboard, while she held in her hand that hateful, ragged red book used for grammar. Then she copied, alternating the green and red colors. Hans could not help watching her. Occasionally he could see that hated smile. She copied:

The glory derived from riches and honors is short and frail.

Youth is the time when the seeds of character are sown.

When she had finished this task she told Hans to bring her the switches. Smiling, she made him stand before her desk.

"You know, Hans, I am going to whip you because you were vulgar, and disobedient." She moistened her smile. "God does not like disobedient boys. He will punish them." Again her tongue came out and moved carefully from one corner of her mouth to the other. "First I want you to say after me: 'Dear Miss Crow, I am sorry.' Begin."

Hans was shaking with hatred, pale and resolute. Not one word would she make him say.

"Begin, I tell you." Silence and a defiant hatred was the only answer he gave her. "Begin, you, you. . . ." Her voice choking with anger, she rose from her seat and began whipping. It didn't hurt much. Those long sticks were a success. Suddenly she stopped, broke both of the sticks in the middle, and putting the two heavy ends together, she began beating his legs and back. Each blow cut his skin until he could endure it no longer. He cried and screamed at the top of his voice.

"Say you are sorry, Hans, say it."

He cried and cried but would not do as she asked. Then she began again with one hand and holding him fast by the wrist with the other. She finally drew blood on his legs below the knees. Under his shirt his back was a mass of large blue welts when finally she turned him loose. His eyes were red with crying, and his heart beat so rapidly that he thought he would die of the pain. He ran out of the door and threw himself in the snow by the roadside, where his brothers, who had been waiting for him, came to pick him up.

He could hardly walk, his legs hurt him so, and his back felt as though it were on fire. Two long, hard miles home, the longest he was ever to walk in his life. As the pain eased a little, he began that systematic and thorough cursing, in which he was considered an artist among boys who were all well trained in this accomplishment. For over a mile, he eased his pain and humiliation by a steady stream of swearing that was often repetitive, but also original in the tortures expressed as fit for Miss Crow.

2

Up to this time she had ruled with an iron hand, but she had not reckoned with the power of Hans and his brothers, nor with their influence in the school, for the manner in which Hans had defied the teacher and been supported in his rebellion by his brothers had given them a brief period of real leadership. Hans, David, and Frank now began a systematic persecution which at first was not exactly a clearly defined plan, but which grew and developed into a campaign designed to torture Miss Crow and make her position unendurable. They began to count the number of times during the day that they could drive that sickening smile from her face. They would spend their evenings in plotting the next day's activities, carefully planning some trick that would disturb her peace of mind.

The first act came easily, almost spontaneously. The next day after the whipping, Miss Crow made special advances to Hans. She asked him to recite first in the reading class. This had formerly been his greatest delight. He read well, and was proud of his voice and accent, and he seldom mispronounced a word. In response to her demand, he stood up to read, but not in his usual manner. Instead, he read in perfect imitation of Johnny Heitmann, one word at a time, in a slow singsong voice, mispronouncing as many words as possible.

"Hans, try that again. You are the best reader in the class." He read again in exactly the same tone of voice.

"Now, Hans, how do you pronounce 'liberty'?"

"Riberty," said Hans, with a sort of mixture of r and l.

"But you can do better than that. Try it again." He repeated his mispronunciation. She saw that he was being obstinate but decided to ignore it.

"Sit down, Hans."

In the History class that followed she called on David.

"David," she said, "who was the leader of the Confederate Army at Gettysburg?"

"Stonewall Jackson," said David in his usual exact tone of voice. For a moment she was startled, for David was infallible in his answers. "No, that is not right. Try again."

"I guess I don't know," he replied.

"Who was the commander of the Northern Army?"

"Longstreet."

"Now, David, you know better than that. Do you want to go to the foot of the class?"

"I don't care," said David.

This form of sabotage provided the students with great amusement, and it helped the Grimsen boys to formulate their plans. Other things happened in their favor. In front of Hans and David sat the dumbest boy in school. He was the Heitmann boy whom Hans had imitated. His nickname was Nosey Johnny, a name that had grown from an exact description of his appearance. He never carried a handkerchief and always wiped his nose with a long, sweeping motion of his arm using the sleeve of his coat as a handkerchief. The sleeves on both arms were shiny with the accumulation of many weeks' service to his ever running nose. David saw the fine possibility of using this boy to torture the teacher. It was a simple matter to get him to wipe his nose at least once during every recitation period. If he should ever forget, David would give him a slight kick on the shins. This never failed to destroy the teacher's smile for an appreciable period of time. As the days passed new schemes were developed that before the winter was over were to bear more fruit than any of the boys had dreamed, when they first began this program of systematic persecution.

3

This united attempt to persecute the teacher had for a time created a greater feeling of harmony between the Grimsen boys and the rest of the students than had ever before existed among them. The intimate feeling that grows among plotters had given these Danish boys their first sense of socially "belonging." Their success in this respect was not without periods when they felt the old atmosphere of social ostracism.

Bert Dance was the son of a rich farmer and landlord who often successfully tortured the younger boys in the school. He liked especially well to pick on Hans and Frank. He would often tell the other children stories he had heard about the Grimsen family, stories that he may have invented or that he had overheard from the conversation of older people. He would tell these stories in front of Hans and Frank, because he knew how deeply they resented them. One day, at the noon hour, he spoke of Hans' mother saying, "You know what she does? When she cuts bread she places the loaf against her bosom and then whittles away until the slice falls on the table. And that ain't all either, they say that in the old country all the Danes eat horse meat."

Hans was so humiliated that he cried. He was used to being tortured in one way or another, but this was the first time anyone had insulted his mother. It was so terrible a thing to Hans that he became sick and had to go home.

When he reached the kitchen that afternoon, and saw his mother, and felt the comfort of the kitchen with the good smell of coffee, he cried again until his mother was worried, believing he really was sick. He couldn't tell her that he was crying for joy. Never before had he loved his mother as he did at that moment. She guessed that something bad had happened at school, but he never told her what it was. His usual cheerfulness returned after coffee, but he stayed in the kitchen with her all afternoon.

Frank shared Hans' hatred for Bert Dance, but he was too young not to be an easy victim of any scheme Bert might invent to torture some child. Bert's connection with wealth and social position was most clearly revealed to the Grimsen boys by the fact that he had a large orange in his dinner pail every day. The sight of an orange in the middle of winter was a wonder to be mentioned at home in the Grimsen family. The only time they had ever had oranges was at the Fourth of July celebration the previous summer.

One day Bert had been watching Frank's longing observation of the orange he was eating. Frank could not keep his eyes from following the marvelous manner in which the orange could be broken off in beautiful, yellow wedge-shaped sections. Finally, Bert said, "Would you like an orange, Frank?"

"Oh, yes, better than anything in the world," he said very quickly, so surprised and excited that he did not even stop to think that there might be a trick involved in Bert's offer.

"Well, I'll tell you what I'll do. If you will feed my horse for me every noon for the rest of this week I'll bring you an orange next Monday."

"Sure, I will. I will do it longer if you want me to," said Frank, for he rather liked Bert's horse.

Bert was the only one who rode a horse to school, and he kept it during the day in a farmer's stable about forty rods from the school grounds. Each noon for the rest of the week, punctually fulfilling his task, Frank cared for Bert's horse.

Hans had heard this bargain made, and thought it fair enough. Twice he had accompanied Frank during the noon hour to the barn to feed the horse, but they had not spoken of the orange. Sunday night when all conversation in bed had ended, and the quiet which precedes sleep had settled over the room, Frank suddenly spoke to Hans, who was lying in the bed beside him.

"Do you think it will be as big as the ones he usually brings for himself?"

Hans answered without a moment's hesitation. "I am sure it will. Didn't he make the offer himself?"

"I am going to give you half of it," said Frank.

"You don't need to do that. I'll be satisfied with a quarter."

"No, I'm going to give you half of it," said Frank.

"That will sure be fine," said Hans.

In the morning when his mother was packing his dinner pail, Frank said, "You don't need to put any cake in mine today."

"Why not? Are you tired of cake?" said his mother, not a little surprised, because Monday morning the children were always delighted, because she had a piece of layer cake saved over from Sunday for each of them. Since this never happened more than once a week, a refusal from Frank was surprising.

"I'm going to have an orange today. Bert Dance promised me one."

"An orange. Well, now that's real nice of him. I told you that there must be more good in him than you boys seem to think."

Frank did not reply. He felt that she was right and his conscience hurt him a little because of all the mean things he had said about Bert.

Noon came. The boys were all sitting around on their desks in a sort of circle. They all knew of the bargain, and were rather envious of Frank. He knew this and could not help feeling a little proud of his advantage.

Sure enough, when Bert Dance opened his dinner pail he took out two oranges instead of one. Both of them were large and beautiful to behold. They were wrapped in a pink tissue paper which was so arranged that only part of the orange showed. It was as though the sweet, delicious fruit nestled lovingly in the soft, pink paper.

They all ate their lunch. Frank finished early, and sat with a careless air, pretending to listen to the conversation. Secretly he was thinking, "Why doesn't he give it to me? He knows I'm through."

Bert said nothing about the orange. He finished his sandwiches, picked up his orange, peeled it and ate. By this time, Frank was getting sick with fear that Bert did not mean to live up to his promise. The older boys were amused, for they sensed the perfect manner in which Bert was torturing Frank. At last Bert picked up the other orange, and made as if to put it into his pail, and then acting surprised he said, "Oh, Frank, this one is for you, isn't it?" He then handed it over.

Frank said, "Thanks," as he took it paper and all in his hands. With nervous fingers he began to remove the paper. The orange fell apart, and he discovered he had two perfect halves in his hands, but they were hollow, not a shred of fruit in them. For a moment everyone in the group gazed with astonishment, and then broke into roaring laughter at the perfect joke Bert had played on Frank.

Frank was too nervous and excited to protest. He fell over in his seat with his face on his forearms and

cried until his body shook with sobs. Hans' heart ached
for his little brother but all he could do was to say to
Bert, "You dirty skunk, I'll get even with you for
this." Bert was so amused over the perfect manner in
which he had played the joke on Frank that he paid
no attention to Hans' insult. He answered only by
saying to the other boys, "All right, let's get outside
and play Fox and Geese."

This little episode did not interfere with the general
program upon which all the boys in the school were
thoroughly united. As time passed they became more
and more conscious of the fact that they did have a
clearly defined objective which was to make life for
the teacher so disagreeable that she would have to give
up the school. They skillfully avoided an open attack
for which she could punish them individually. There
were a multitude of things that could be done secretly
with the appearance of being accidental.

One day while a group of them were standing
around the water pail a boy tied a string to the pail and
attached it also to a buttonhole of his coat. When they
all turned away from the pail it was pulled over and
the water spilled on the floor. The boy, of course,
claimed that he was innocent, that one of the others
had tied the string. Miss Crow did not even try to
question them, for she knew that it would be impossible
to get a confession.

When she left the room at the recess times or at the
noon hour, she would often return to find dirty four-
letter words printed on the blackboard. Often when the

boys were marching into school keeping step to her beating of the time one of them would pretend to slip and fall down. All the others would then break line as though they were much concerned about the boy who had fallen. While putting coal in the stove they would drop the coal bucket and attract the attention of the whole school.

As time passed these devices multiplied in number until the teacher became so nervous that she could scarcely conduct her classes. She pleaded with them one day to co-operate with her, and offered to post on the blackboard the names of the students who gave the best recitations and had the most perfect behavior mark. They listened in silence, but not one responded to her plea. Already they had sensed their power over her. She had stopped her usual round of punishments in the hope that what she couldn't win by force she might gain by pleading.

One day the County Superintendent visited the school. It had always been Miss Crow's practice on the occasions of this official visit to call on the boys who could give the best account of their work in order to show the superintendent how well her students were progressing. Thus she had never failed to ask the Grimsen boys to recite, nor had they ever failed in the past. On this particular visit she followed the usual procedure, only to be met with a polite but complete refusal of co-operation. Alfred claimed he hadn't read his lesson, David gave wrong answers to all the questions that were asked of him. Hans was requested to work a problem in long division for the class at the blackboard, but he failed to get the right answer. When she said "You know Hans that you must always bring down one figure after each time you subtract," he answered, "You never told me that before." Even then he pretended that he couldn't get the right answer. Other boys claimed that she was asking them to recite on an assignment she had never given them, until by the time noon came, she had scarcely received one correct answer from her pupils.

This, however, was only the beginning of the shocks she was to receive on that day. There was one place on this school ground which she never visited, and her experience in town teaching had not taught her to consider it as a part of her program. This little white building that stood at the back and in one corner of the school yard was left without supervision to the boys' own rule. As the dissatisfaction with Miss Crow had increased, all sorts of destructive activities had spread from the school room to other parts of the school property, but nowhere had it shown itself more than in this particular spot.

The boys kicked many boards off on the side away from the school. This gave an open view into the orchard at the back. They broke the seats, and tore the door loose from the hinges, and in many other ways less pleasant to the eye they made this retreat almost unfit for its purpose. Even as they added to their acts of vandalism, the growing contradictions of their actions became clear to them. It was as though they were compelled by a power beyond their control to destroy that which they prized most of all.

Here they often gathered in small groups to talk of secret things and to exchange confidences that were not for the ears of all. Uncomfortable as the place was, it had an atmosphere of freedom—it was a sort of sacred, untouchable spot in the midst of the general tyranny that reigned on the playground and in the schoolroom. As the battered door closed, the dominating presence of the teacher faded away. Here the spirit was free from the power that ruled outside, free to speak out in thought and action. It was a sanctuary to the persecuted, a place guarded from the enemies' attack by the iron bands of custom,—a power stronger than deep moats or barbed wire.

As the cold north winds shrieked over the dead corn stalks, it also whistled through openings in the boys' shelter. They had prepared a scene of destruction for the visiting superintendent, but they had also deprived themselves of comfort in their last refuge. Their suppressed dissatisfaction had reached the point where it was injuring those who rebelled as much as the object against which they wished to exercise their anger. The whole thing was purposeless, cruel and without direction.

As soon as the school was dismissed for the noon period, the boys watched with nervous excitement and some fear, as the Superintendent crossed the yard and entered the "little house." In a moment he came rushing out again. His fat face was red with fury as he stormed across the yard. He came directly up to the boys who had gathered around the front porch, and spoke to them:

"Never in all my days as Superintendent have I seen a worse group of dirty, misbehaved boys than I find here. You may think you are smart, but I'm going to tell you one thing. I'm going to write to your parents, and I'm also going to let them know there is a law against wilful destruction of state property. If you don't have that house repaired next time I come, every board in place, I say, I'll have you fined. Most of you know what you'll get at home if your fathers have to pay a fine for what you have done. Now you can all go home for today, and tell your parents why I sent you home. I'm going to have a talk with your teacher. If she can't handle you I'll make arrangements for someone to help her who can take care of you. Do you understand? Now get your dinner pails and go straight home."

This was something they had not figured into their program. None of them wanted to have the task of explaining why they were coming home in the middle of the day, and none of them told their parents the truth.

What the Superintendent told Miss Crow none of them ever knew, but they did know that the help he promised her never came. She attempted to regain her power, but as soon as she settled one evil, another came to take its place. She made the boys repair the "little house," which they were only too glad to do, but this error corrected gave birth to another.

All sorts of petty, mean persecutions followed one another in rapid succession. As the teacher lost control, the inventive power of the schoolchildren increased. Not a day passed without some new trick to disrupt the discipline in the school room. Mass protest had spread to include the girls, until there was almost no discipline at all. With the spread of revolt grew a general disregard for the person of the teacher herself. One day as school was dismissed for the noon recess, someone shouted a vile word at the teacher as he ran from the room.

This was the end. Miss Crow told the pupils who were still in the room that school was over and that they should go home. She then locked the doors. Two of the girls were crying, for they knew what was wrong. Miss Crow stopped to speak to them, and then she too cried. The boys saw her wiping her eyes as she walked off the corner of the lot, never to return.

Some of the boys were conscience stricken when they saw what had really been the outcome of these two months of violent persecution. For them it had all been an exciting game. They had planned for the particular effect they achieved, but they had been quite unaware of the extent to which they had succeeded in torturing their teacher. Even Hans and his brothers, who wanted revenge, were a little terrified by the final outcome.

Soon the children were scattered along the roads in

four directions from the school house. They were walking in groups of twos or more, but there was little conversation. Many of them had not even stopped to eat their lunch. This was true of the Grimsen boys, who had cut through the corn field in order that they might be alone. They walked slowly, without speaking for a long time. Finally Hans said, "Why didn't she treat us right? It wasn't our fault that she got into trouble."

"I'm glad she is gone," said Frank.

IX

"Hans, Hans, wake up!"

Hans opened his eyes, and saw his father leaning over the bed, holding a lantern in his hand. Hans glanced at the table, wondering if he had left any signs of tobacco lying around.

"Hans, get up. The big sow can't get her pigs."

It was after midnight in the middle of April. Peter Grimsen had fifteen brood sows bred for spring furrowing. His lack of information on cross breeding had led him to cross Duroc Jerseys and Poland Chinas. He had hoped to combine the large frame of the one with the capacity for fatness of the other. He did not know that such a cross usually resulted in the sow's inability to give birth to her litter. The pig in the womb grew too large for natural delivery.

Hans was not surprised when he heard his father explain his reason for this midnight visit to the bedroom. Just the day before the same trouble had occurred in connection with one of the other sows. Peter Grimsen had at that time sent word to town with a neighbor asking the veterinarian to call. When the veterinarian arrived, he claimed that the only solution would be to use a forceps. This he did, but he handled his instrument so unskillfully that he injured the walls of the uterus. The pigs were delivered, a full dozen of them, and six of these were living. They were kept in a box well lined with straw back of the kitchen stove. Each one had its own separate bottle with a nipple. The boys helped Meta feed them, for the sow had been so severely injured that it was quite plain she would die. She had lain quietly in her pen ever since the delivery, unable to move, and unwilling to take even a drink of water.

It was not only the coming death of this one sow that disturbed Peter and kept him in the hog house all night long. The veterinarian told him of the dangerous nature of the crossbreeding Peter had tried, and he also said that all of the sows would have the same trouble as the first one and that most of them would probably die.

All day and all night Peter had wrestled with this bit of news. He thought of all the ways by which he might have avoided this particular crossbreeding. He thought of how it was the merest accident of his stopping to talk with a farmer one day on his way home from town, and how the man had asked him in to see his pigs. Peter ended the brief visit by buying a young boar, because he seemed to be such a fine animal. And now it had all come to this. If he had only enquired from some of the older farmers, they could have told him. "But in God's name," as he said to Meta, "how could I know that it is not safe to cross certain breeds. Tell me that." Meta had said, "No, of course not, Peter." No, he could not have known. There were so many things to know in this land, and he walked from the kitchen back to the hog house, which had now been enlarged in spite of the trouble with the landlord. He stood there by the hour. Here were the hogs that should more than pay for the new hog house condemned to die. That's what the veterinarian said.

Not only were the hogs to pay for the new building, but they were also to carry the increase in rent which he was now forced to pay the landlord. Many times during the winter he had figured his profits. Even if his sows should average only eight pigs each, and they might easily average ten, eight times fifteen would be one hundred and twenty pigs at fifteen dollars each . . . and so on it would go. Now the veterinarian had practically doomed all his brood sows to death. Before leaving he sold Peter a pair of forceps and gave him simple instructions in the technique of their use. He gave the instructions to Peter, but it was Hans who stood by listening and learning.

2

The second sow began labor at ten that night. All of Peter's efforts with the forceps had failed, so now he was calling Hans, whose small but strong and active hands might prove more effective than the forceps.

"You must hurry Hans, and help me with the sow. She can't get her pigs. I want you to see if you can pull them by hand."

In the kitchen his mother had a big cup of coffee and a piece of cake ready for him.

"Are you awfully sleepy, Hans?"

"Oh no, not so sleepy, but still I'm sleepy. It is so cold upstairs."

"Now, hurry, Hans," said his father. "Here, put this sweater on, and here is a pail of lard to take with you. You'll need to grease your hands good."

"If you can save the sows for me, you can have one of the little pigs for yourself," said Peter.

"Yes, I know," said Hans. He knew how that would be: Hans' pig, but father's hog when it was ready for the market. He used to believe in that, too.

Down in the hog house the air was warm and pungent with the not unpleasant odors of the hogs and straw. Hans rolled his right sleeve to the shoulder, and after greasing his arm thoroughly with lard, he made his first attempt.

"How damnably slippery these pigs are," he thought. Over and over again he could catch hold, and then lose his grip as soon as he began to pull.

"You must learn to pull when the sow labors," said his father.

"Yes, that seems to work better."

After fifteen minutes he brought out the first pig. A sense of achievement elated him. This was not so bad. He pulled the afterbirth off its head and placed the little pig by the sow's teats. Then he began to try for the second. His father stood by the side of the pen smoking his pipe and holding the lantern. The dim flame cast a weird glow over the rather grim scene. There was no sound except the grunting of the sow that followed each period of labor. She lay flat on her side, but as she tried to force the pigs out of the womb she turned almost over on her back.

Hans began to perspire. The straw in which he knelt, or at times almost lay down, was wet from the birth fluids. It soaked into his clothes.

He was conscious of his father's presence. Somehow this annoyed him. He was nearly always annoyed when he had to work with his father.

"If ever a fellow needed a chew, I need one now," he thought. "Dad, why don't you hang the lantern on a nail and go to bed? You can't help me, anyway."

"I'd just as soon stay here, son. You might not like to be alone."

"Oh, I'd rather be alone. This is particular work, and I can do it better by myself."

This amused his father, but he saw that it might be better if he would leave. He hung the lantern on the wall.

"All right, I'll go to bed, then, and get a little sleep before morning. You call me if you have any trouble."

Left to himself, Hans put a large chew in his mouth and returned to his task. It struck him that this was not only unusual work, but it was fascinating in character as well. He began to have a deep feeling of sympathy for the helpless animal that lay suffering by his side. His heart beat with sympathy for her. He realized as he never had before, his kinship with the hogs that were despised as the lowest of animals.

There was something almost human in the relationship that here existed in the dead quiet of night, in a hog pen, on a lonely farm. Two pigs had now been delivered—cute little crawling things, living and breathing.

The prophet in the desert, under the starry sky, may feel something of the mystery of life, and of man's yearning for God, or for meaning, or significance in the universe. To Hans, this experience in the hog pen partook, in its own strange way, of that same quality. For all that sense-evidence had to offer, he was alone in the great, vast, black, silent universe. With the sensitiveness to particular places that is so important to the psychology of childhood, he was alive in every nerve to his surroundings and his task. All that was unpleasant about it had long since ceased to concern him. A vast, silent loneliness and boundless sympathy existed between him and the suffering animal at his side. The pain and sorrow of the world was for Hans that night symbolized in his task. His passion for justice, friendship and understanding was by some strange alchemy of circumstance a living reality on this night.

He worked steadily until at last nine pigs, all alive, lay at their mother's side. He watched carefully for further signs of labor, but none seemed to appear. Yet he could not be sure, nor could anything have persuaded him to leave until he had finished. He piled some fresh straw against the side of the pen so that he could lie down to rest for a few moments.

His brother found him there in the morning, peacefully sleeping. Beside him lay the sow, grunting those rather fast, regular little grunts that signify she is giving milk. At her side were nine little pigs all enjoying their breakfast.

The ludicrousness of this scene was often a subject for joking in the family. Hans knew better than to try to explain the inexplicable. He had faced a new kind of reality that night which exalted him, made him know better than he had ever known before the meaning of life, but it was a meaning that was emotional in its nature, not easily defined by the limitations of logic or reason.

3

All through the month of April, as one sow after another began labor, Hans worked at his task. Sometimes it was during the day, but mostly at night, and always he worked alone. Since the teacher had been run out by the pupils, no new one had been elected. The board had decided to close the school for the remainder of the year. Thus it was that Hans was free to work with the sows. The great success of his first night was not often repeated. By the time it was all over, seven out of the fifteen brood sows had died, and instead of one hundred and twenty pigs as Peter had counted, there were only sixty-four.

The eight sows that had died were cut up and the fattest parts were melted into lard, from which Meta made soap for laundry purposes. The parts that could not be made into soap were fed to the chickens or burned.

It was a sad business for Peter to see his fine brood sows made into soap or burned. Every day when he walked through the long hog house that he had built, he saw the empty pens, pens that had only a month before held so much promise.

"Well, if the corn is a good price this year, it will bring me almost as much as it would if I put it through the hogs," he thought. He was trying to make himself forget that corn usually brought twice the market price when fed to hogs or cattle.

4

When August came, there were rumors that hog-cholera was spreading among the farms east of town. Then it became a reality. Every day someone brought news of another farmer whose hogs were dying of cholera. A great fear settled over the community. Had this plague affected human beings, it could scarcely have produced a more ominous social atmosphere. Farmers made hurried trips to town for needed supplies, remaining only to exchange a few words of conversation on the latest cholera outbreak. As soon as they came home, their first act was to visit the hog pen, where they would stand looking long and earnestly at every single hog to see if any signs of the cholera had appeared.

There was no scientific preventive known for hog

cholera in those days, but all sorts of queer practices were tried. One of Peter's neighbors told him that there was an old negress near Lincoln who could destroy the cholera by burning some strange herbs in the hog yard. "I heard," he added, "that a man over by Murdock used her treatment and not a single one of his hogs died."

"No?" said Peter. "Neither have mine, yet."

5

One day an old friend of the Grimsens drove into the yard. His name was Thorwald Simonsen, and among the Danes he was known as The Giant. No one ever knew why he had left Denmark with his wife, two sons and two daughters, to settle on a small farm near Weeping Willow but that there was *something* they did know.

He was a man of character, who ruled his family with an iron hand. When he said to one of his children, "You may go to town tonight, but you must be home by ten o'clock," he meant ten o'clock and not five minutes after.

Once in his early years in the Weeping Willow settlement, he had become well known for his dealings with the banker. It happened one day while he was doing his morning chores, that a neighbor came rushing into his yard shouting, "Mr. Simonsen, the bank has failed. All our savings are lost. They say we can't get a cent of our money."

Mr. Simonsen finished pouring the slop into the hog trough, set the pail carefully in its place, then, turning to his neighbor, he said, "Do you say we can't get our money? It's our money, isn't it?"

"Yes, but they say the door of the bank was locked yesterday afternoon, and that the bank has failed."

"Failed? You talk drivel and nonsense. I intend to get my money."

"What will you do? How will you get it? I am driving in now. Do you want to go with me? I am going right now. The boys are hitching up for me."

"No, thank you, I can't go just now. I had planned to spend an hour this morning repairing a few things around the barn, but I'll come to town for my money later."

"You should hurry, Mr. Simonsen."

"No, I should not hurry. I shall come when I am ready and not earlier."

He completed the work he had planned for the hour, then went into the house, washed his hands and face, and put on a clean pair of overalls.

"Where are you going, Thorwald?" asked his wife.

"I have heard that the bank has failed. I am going to town to get my money."

"The bank failed! Then all our savings are lost! Oh, what shall we do now? Everything we have saved is gone!" She burst into tears.

"Be still, will you? I told you I was going to get the money, didn't I? Then be still."

He left the house and hitched his horses to the buggy. When he reached Weeping Willow, he saw a crowd gathered around the bank.

"Here comes Mr. Simonsen," said one of the bystanders, "He has said that he is going to get his money."

"How are you going to do it, Mr. Simonsen?" shouted one.

"There is no one there," said another.

"Are you going to blow the safe?" said a third, trying to be jocular.

There was a touch of jeering in their remarks, because the bench-sitters of Weeping Willow who made up the majority of those present did not like Mr. Simonsen any too well. He never joined them in their idle gossip. When he came to town, he came on business. That completed, he returned home. Now all were taking a rather savage delight in seeing The Giant defeated, at least once in his life.

Mr. Simonsen walked up the steps and looked through the glass door. The bank was empty. The door of the safe was locked. He turned around and walked away.

"Why don't you go in, Mr. Simonsen?" someone shouted.

"He's just another one of them there goddam Danes that think they can do what they want to," said another. But he said it carefully, after The Giant was out of hearing.

The Giant was six feet four inches tall, and muscular. When he loaded his hogs for market, he lifted them into the wagon. It was known that he could lift a three-hundred pound squirming hog as easily as another man could handle a sack of wheat.

Now they watched his deliberate, unhurried walk. His bushy black beard, two feet long, blew back in the breeze across his shoulders.

Mr. Simonsen walked to the banker's house which was about six blocks from the bank, in a secluded, shady grove. He knocked at the door. A hired girl appeared.

"I want to see Mr. Harkins."

"He does not want to see anyone today," replied the girl.

Mr. Simonsen took hold of the screen door and opened it. It was as though he only touched it with his hand, but the hook that held it popped out of the wood with a quick snap.

"Do I have to walk into his house, or will you tell him that I want to see him?"

"Oh, yes, I'll tell him," she said, almost running from the hall.

In a moment Mr. Harkins appeared. He was a small, skinny man, about five feet six inches tall. He was clean shaven, wore glasses, and spoke in a quick, nervous manner. For years he had been speculating with the farmers' money, flattering them in a patronizing tone whenever they entered the bank. Today he was excited.

"Good day, Mr. Simonsen. And what can I do for you today?"

"I thought I would just come in and get my money."

"But you know, the examiner closed the bank yesterday afternoon. I am awfully sorry but. . . ."

"I said I came in to get my money. Will you be so good as to come down to the bank and get it for me?" repeated Mr. Simonsen in his characteristic, low, even tones.

"You don't understand, Mr. Simonsen," began the banker, falling into that superior tone of voice he always used when talking to these "ignorant" Danish farmers. When they came to him for help he never failed to lecture them about the difficulties of lending money without security. There was nothing he liked better than to keep a farmer standing helpless at his window while he explained to him the rules and regulations governing a loan.

"You see the law will not. . . ."

"I am not here to talk to you about the law. I came to ask you to be so kind as to come with me to the bank. I have four hundred and fifty-two dollars and twenty-five cents on deposit there. I would like to draw it all out."

The banker felt he was being insulted, and now assumed his most superior tone.

"You Danes can never understand anything. Can't you see that I am not able to do what you ask?"

"No, we can't understand anything, but will you try to understand that I want my money, now?"

He reached over and grasped Mr. Harkins under

the arms, letting his powerful hands grip clothes and skin, and lifted him two feet off the ground and shook him as a dog shakes a rat. He shook him until his glasses flew off, and then he said, "Can you understand now, Mr. Harkins, that I want my money, or do I have to use other means?"

"Yes, but. . . ."

He shook him again until his feet dangled against the wall.

"Could you, Mr. Harkins, come down to the bank with me, without any more 'buts'?"

"Yes," said Mr. Harkins in a weak, scared voice.

The Giant set him on the floor, but kept one hand on his shoulder. Mr. Harkins stooped and picked up his glasses. He then rubbed his sides, first the one and then the other. He felt as though all the skin had been torn loose in that terrific grasp.

"Here is your hat, Mr. Harkins. Now let us go."

As they walked down the street, the banker again began to explain. This time Mr. Simonsen let him talk. As they drew nearer and nearer to the bank, Mr. Harkins grew more and more nervous. He could see the group gathered on the sidewalk.

"So don't you see, Mr. Simonsen," he almost pleaded, "I can't really do anything for you," and with that he stopped.

They were on a corner of the street just one block from the bank.

"Shall I pick you up again?" said Mr. Simonsen, and he laid a heavy hand on his shoulder.

"No, no, but can't you see. . . ." The heavy hand closed on his shoulder near his neck as though it would crush his collar bone. The banker, with difficulty, suppressed a scream of pain.

"Shall we go?"

"Yes! Yes!"

The crowd by the bank was shocked into silence when they saw this strange pair coming up the street. The banker unlocked the door and both went inside. The door was again locked before the crowd thought to move. Then they surged to the glass door to watch.

They saw Mr. Harkins open the safe and bring a roll of bills and change to the cashier's window. Then they observed a brief argument, but only for a minute. Mr. Simonsen handed over his bank book and received a roll of bills and some small change. The banker returned the remainder of the money to the safe and locked the door. He then walked with his customer to the front door. Again he seemed to be pleading unsuccessfully. Mr. Simonsen opened the door. The crowd made way for him, and in so doing, cleared the doorway entrance long enough for the banker to slam the door.

"Is he going to open the bank?"

"Did he let you have it all?"

Other questions were shouted at Mr. Simonsen, but he made no answer, nor did he act as though he saw the crowd about him.

At last someone shouted, "He ran out the back door!" The few moments that elapsed while the crowd was trying to find out from Mr. Simonsen what had happened in the bank gave Mr. Harkins the opportunity to plan his escape.

Mr. Simonsen got into his buggy which was near the front of the bank. As he started to back away from the hitching rack, he saw the banker come out of the front door and run across the street toward the railroad tracks. His going out the back door was a successful ruse which led all the people in front of the bank to run to the end of the block and down the alley.

"So now he is running away," thought Mr. Simonsen.

And he was right. Mr. Harkins caught a train out of Weeping Willow that very morning.

6

That was long ago. Today The Giant came driving into Peter Grimsen's yard. His long, heavy beard was almost snow white now, for he had aged greatly in the last years. Crop failures and the break-up of his family had left their marks.

As Peter hurried from the barn to greet his visitor, he could not but observe the quiet way in which Mr. Simonsen kept sitting in the buggy. Peter thought, "He has been taking his son's absence pretty hard. The dirty preacher was to blame for all that."

One of Simonsen's sons had been engaged to the daughter of a neighboring farmer. Mr. Simonsen had not exactly approved of her, but he had not openly interfered, although he disliked his neighbor because he was a lazy, slovenly person, whose land was never properly farmed. Still, Mr. Simonsen did not feel that he could honestly object to the girl on this score, and so the affair had drifted along until his son became engaged to her.

One morning, while Mr. Simonsen was working in the yard, his neighbor appeared. After a little preliminary talk about the weather and the corn, the neighbor, whose name was Madsen, said, "It was about Elsa, that I came."

"About Elsa?" said Mr. Simonsen in a questioning tone.

"Yes. You see she is not so well. That is, my wife is worried about her. We are ashamed, too, but then such things happen. Only we had not thought it of your son. And now my wife said I must tell you, and I am sorry too, but after all, she is my daughter."

Mr. Simonsen did not show the distress he felt, and when he spoke his voice was as calm as if the subject of the weather had not been changed. "You mean then. . . ."

"Yes. It's the truth," said Madsen interrupting before Mr. Simonsen could finish his sentence.

"This is hard for me to believe. I shall go to the field now and talk to him."

"Yes, do that," said Madsen, feeling he must say something, even though he knew it would not mean anything to his neighbor.

"If my son is guilty, he will marry her, but he will

also leave my house, do you hear? I will come back to see you."

With these words he turned his back and started for the field where his son was cultivating corn.

It was not long until Madsen, who had returned to his home, saw Mr. Simonsen striding into the yard. Without a word of greeting he spoke, "Where is your daughter, Elsa?"

"She is in the house."

"Tell her to come here."

In a moment Elsa appeared. She was a pretty blonde with curly hair, and a soft, delicate mouth. It was clear that she had been crying. Inside the house by the window, her mother was watching and wiping her eyes.

"Elsa," said Mr. Simonsen in his clear, quiet tone, "Will you tell me the truth?"

She looked at the ground, but did not speak.

Her father was looking in the other direction, and he saw that Mr. Simonsen's son had unhitched his team and was now almost in his father's yard with the horses.

"Can this mean he is coming to marry her now?" he thought.

"Look at me, Elsa. Will you tell me the truth? Answer me."

"Yes, I will." And then she sat down on the steps of the porch and began to cry.

"Now, now, daughter," said her father, "you mustn't cry. This is a bad thing you have done, but we can forgive you if you will tell us the truth." He was not at all displeased that his daughter would be marrying the son of so well-to-do a farmer as Mr. Simonsen.

"Just answer Mr. Simonsen."

"Elsa, my son says that he is not responsible for your shame. Has he told me the truth?"

Through her tears she said, "Yes."

"What, you slut, you disgraceful child, what are you saying?" shouted her father. He was wild with rage. He grabbed her by the hair and pulled her screaming to an upright position.

"Who was it, then? Tell me before I beat you."

"It was the Reverend Wheat."

"The Reverend Wheat," gasped Mr. Simonsen, for this was enough of a shock to disturb his composure for a moment, "and I have had him as a guest in my house many and many a time."

"You slut," again screamed her father, and while he held her by the hair with one hand, he smote her across the face with the other, and then threw her with violence into the dirt at his feet.

Mr. Simonsen walked out of the yard more disturbed than he was willing to admit even to himself. When he turned to close the gate, he saw the girl's mother kneeling by the side of her pregnant daughter in the dust of the farmyard.

As he neared the driveway to his own yard, he saw his son dressed in Sunday clothes, drive down the road toward town at a furious pace.

"Now, what can this mean?" he thought.

In the kitchen he found his wife weeping.

"Why, mother, what is the matter?"

"I don't know. He said to ask you."

"Where is he going?"

"I don't know, but he kissed me, and then said good-bye. What has he done? What is the matter?"

He then explained the events of the morning.

That afternoon a neighbor boy drove Mr. Simonsen's team into the yard, explaining that he had been asked to take the team home. That was all.

Three weeks later, a letter came from New York City, and Mr. Simonsen learned that his son had joined the army that was getting ready to invade Cuba. He wrote not a single word about Elsa.

7

"Good-day, Thorwald. I am glad to see you."

"Good-day, Peter," said Thorwald, and then he laughed. It was not a loud, hearty laugh, but more of a soft chuckle that seemed to perpetuate itself.

"Come, get off the seat. Why do you have that heifer tied to your buggy?"

"Why?" replied Mr. Simonsen. "You bought her, didn't you?"

"What can be the matter with Thorwald today?" thought Peter. Is he trying to joke or what is it?

"No, I didn't buy her. But I wouldn't mind having her. What do you want for her?"

The Giant looked puzzled.

"Is that the truth, Peter? Didn't you buy her?"

"No, of course I didn't."

"Hum, hum, so you didn't buy her."

He then turned in his seat and looked carefully in every direction as though he had some secret to impart. He leaned over near to Peter and said, "Tell me, Peter, who bought her? Someone bought her, but I can't remember. I have such a damnable headache."

Peter was profoundly shocked. Thorwald was one of his very best friends. It was plain that something was wrong with him. "Can it be that he is out of his mind?" said Peter to himself. He was at a loss to know what to do. He thought of calling Meta, but decided against that, fearing Mr. Simonsen would only grow more nervous. At least he could change the subject, "How are your hogs, Thorwald? Are they all well?"

Then Thorwald laughed again that same quiet, infectious laugh. "I had five left when I started over here. The other forty are dead. The fire has burned steadily now for a week. Some days five of them, some days even more. But it will soon be over now."

"No, you don't tell me! All of them gone? That is awful. But don't take it too hard, Thorwald. It could have been worse." Peter was deeply shocked. He knew what it meant to lose one's hogs, but that it should bring a man to this state, that was taking it too hard.

Thorwald only laughed. "Yes, I could have heard that my son was killed."

"Your son, Thorwald, but why should he be killed. He is still on a farm in Iowa is he not?"

"Iowa?" he answered in a questioning tone. "Iowa? Oh, yes. That's what my wife told me. But I know she is trying to fool me. I know he is in the army in Cuba. He will be killed or die of disease as so many of the others have."

"No, no, Thorwald, that is already long ago. Why that war ended the year I came to Nebraska. Don't you remember that?"

"Peter, are you trying to fool me too? I know that my son will be killed in that war and all because of that skunk of a preacher who ruined Elsa. She was not such a bad girl for my son if all could have gone well with them."

This conversation seemed to have quieted him somewhat, for he began to unhitch the team. Peter helped him, and it was not long until the horses were in the barn and they were walking toward the house where the coffee would be ready for them. As they passed the wagon, they stopped to look at the heifer.

Suddenly Thorwald said, "I know. It was my son-in-law who bought the heifer. It was foolish of me to bother you. I am sorry. I must get the horses out again."

"Yes, yes, Thorwald, but come in for a cup of coffee first."

"No, I am deeply sorry, but I must go immediately."

Nothing that Peter could say would change his mind. The horses were brought out and hitched to the wagon.

"Good-bye, Peter, come and see us soon," and chuckling to himself he drove out of the yard. When he reached the road, Peter saw that he turned west instead of east. His son-in-law lived east of Grimsen's place.

Peter shook his head sadly. "What a land this is," he said out loud as he turned toward the house.

8

Before the week was over, the stench of burning flesh rose from Peter Grimsen's farm. Day after day through the hot August weather, Hans and David hitched horses to dead hogs and dragged them to the fire down in the pasture. Oftentimes there would be a brief day of respite and hope that the dreaded plague was over, and then it would begin again.

The melted lard ran down the hillside. The smell of burning hogs grew sickening. Day and night, it was everywhere. The horses would refuse to drink from the water trough until they were almost crazy with thirst. Crows circled all day over the smoldering fire. At night the dogs could be heard fighting and barking down by the burnt hog meat, and the ground was thick with rats there after dark.

In the house no laughter was ever heard. Even the smallest child sensed the presence of some great calamity. Every day the food stood on the table only half eaten, while Peter scolded his children for not cleaning up their plates; scolded, while his own food lay untasted. Then the little children cried, and Meta had to interfere.

"Good Lord, Peter, the children can't help it. Try to be reasonable."

And then there would be quiet, but no more food eaten at that meal.

At last the end came. Peter had nine hogs left when the ravages of cholera ceased. Nine hogs, and he had once counted on at least one hundred and twenty. This was a devil's life, he thought to himself—a very devil's life. What should he do now? He would have to look for another farm if things kept going on like this. He would never be able to pay the increased rent with all the debts that were piling up day after day.

There were days when he never even spoke to Meta, and night after night he paced the floor, back and forth, back and forth, with his hands clasped behind his back. The children did not dare to laugh when he was in the house. But there was an upstairs room, crowded, narrow, with plastered walls that had even more holes than the walls in the parlor. This was the haven of all the older boys. Here they could talk, chew tobacco and read. This was a sanctuary for them. Only once a year on the average did their father invade this retreat. Why this was they never knew. They often wondered, but they never knew.

Once he had been invited to a social at the Congregational church, but he had refused.

"Why don't you go, Alfred," said Meta, "you might get acquainted with a lot of people your own age."

"You know why I won't go. Do you think I would show myself in town wearing pants that stop half way up my legs?"

Then Peter interrupted, "No, of course he won't. He's a rich man's son. He has to have new clothes to go to church. Other people's children can go to such places and enjoy themselves, but not mine. My children are too proud to budge off the place unless it be in the company of the worst, good-for-nothing loafers. His clothes are good enough to go, God only knows where with those drunken tramps in Weeping Willow, but when nice people ask him to go to a party, his clothes aren't good enough."

Alfred left the table and went upstairs. He held his head high. Not one tear did he ever shed in the presence of his father or mother, nor by himself either. A dry-eyed hatred consumed him. He threw himself across the bed, buried his face in the pillow, and pitied himself, but he did not cry.

Peter continued his scolding, but it was only to relieve his own nerves. Meta understood that and said nothing. They never talked about Alfred any more, for although Meta often wanted to she did not dare to bring up the subject, for if she did Peter always blamed her for being too indulgent. Peter would not admit that his son was growing up, and that he had no opportunity for healthy social relations with other young people of his own age. None of the Grimsen boys had ever been invited to parties for young people in their neighborhood, and while there were social gatherings for the young among the Danes it so happened that these were all among the older and more well-to-do settlers east of town. Even if Alfred had been invited he could not have gone, for one could not drive to a party in a lumber wagon.

As the winter wore on Alfred found the only companionship the community offered him. He had always preferred the company of older people and now he began to be welcomed into a group that gathered at the bachelor Polk's house to play penny-ante poker. Often they played only for matches, since money was too scarce, but sometimes they played for money, and Alfred was able to join those games too, for occasionally he would get a day's work scooping corn for some neighbor who would rather pay for help than take it on exchange as nearly all the farmers did.

At these games there was often whiskey, and it was not long until he felt that he had become a real man. He was more mature than most boys of his age, and his background of reading in history and geography often gave him an opportunity to tell these people stories about the past to which they listened with childish interest. They listened partly because they admired what they thought was the great learning of this boy and partly because he had a real gift for expression.

These meetings which were sometimes long evenings of discussion and sometimes card games, bolstered his ego and for a time ended his moody unhappiness.

It was not long until first one and then another of these older people, some of them married men, began to take him along to town on Saturday, and then one night in early spring when Alfred was fifteen, he was taken for the first time to a house of prostitution. He was fifteen and everybody in this crowd was proud of him. "You're a full grown man, now," they said.

But that night he drank more whiskey than he could hold. When he came into his home he stumbled over a chair in the kitchen and finally fell at the foot of the stairs. There Peter found him, sick and vomiting when he came running to see what had caused all the noise. He had to carry his drunken son to bed. To scold him was futile. Even Peter could see that. But he could scold Meta and lay the blame on her. It was not that he really blamed Meta, it was just that he must vent his fury on someone. Wherever he turned, he seemed to be met by some unreasoning force that turned his good intentions into such miserable defeat.

3

In the morning a terrible quarrel developed between Peter and his son. Peter began as soon as Alfred, red-eyed and sick at his stomach, reached the kitchen.

"Where were you last night?"

"In Weeping Willow."

"Where else? Who were you with?"

"I was with Jack Forest, and Ernest Downing."

"What did you do?"

"Do? What do you mean?" Alfred had never before opposed his father, nor had any of the children ever thought of such a thing, but the new company, and the sense of guilt which he could excuse to himself only by being defiant made him oppose his father.

There was a tenseness in the room that even Hobson felt in his place under the table, begging pancakes as was his custom. Bounce wouldn't stay under the table but got up on a chair in the corner of the room where she sat looking as grave as a preacher.

"You know what I mean. Don't talk back to me. What did you do last night?"

"Nothing," said Alfred.

"What do you mean, nothing. You came home drunk. You tell me where you got the whiskey or I'll thrash you."

"No, you won't."

What was this? Was Alfred rebelling? The younger boys trembled, and stopped eating their pancakes. Their mother left the room, but this they did not dare to do, for they would have to pass their father who stood by the door.

Peter's face grew red with anger. He had never been crossed before in his own house. He thundered at Alfred.

"You defy your own father. You not only get drunk, but you defy your own father. Next you will insult

your mother. There is nothing too low for you to do.
You set a nice example for your young brothers. Oh,
that I should live to see the day that a son of mine is a
drunken sot, a liar, a boy who defies his father, insults
his mother and brings all of us to shame! Oh, that I
had sunk into my grave before I was to see this. How
can I go to town again without casting my eyes on the
ground at every step I take? My honor is ruined. I had
better move away from here and give up everything
that I have worked for all these years, for I cannot face
the shame of this. You ungrateful swine of a son. After
all your mother and I have done for you, slaved for
you, saved for you, and now your reward to us is that
you become a drunkard, and parade your shame on the
streets of Weeping Willow and come home to defy
your father."

Alfred was now thoroughly aroused. He saw that in
spite of all his father's talking, that he would not dare
to whip him. He saw with bitter irony the absurdity of
much that his father said, and with the cruelty of youth
he answered back, challenging him.

"Yes, what have you done for me? Do I have a
decent suit of clothes? Do I? Don't I have to wear
pants that are so short they stop at my ankles? I work
every day like a man in the goddam corn fields, and I
can't even have a new suit."

"Don't talk like that to me. Go away. Get out of my
house. And the rest of you with him. Out to the chores.
Go."

They left, the little ones almost running out of the

house. Peter sat at the table, pale, sick, exhausted. Meta came in and poured him a cup of coffee. She spoke to him quietly:

"I believe we'll have to get Alfred a new suit, when we sell the corn this spring."

"Yes, I think so, but I don't know what to do with him now. Why is he like that? He never goes with boys his own age. If he's not with that drunken crowd in Weeping Willow, then he's up at old man Hayden's talking with him about the Civil War. I don't understand him."

"No, I don't either, but I think we had better see that he has a new suit."

4

One scene followed another throughout the summer, for there was now scarcely a Saturday night that Alfred did not go to town with the new friends he had made during the winter. Mr. Hansen, the grocery man, warned Peter of what was happening, thinking that Peter did not know, but that only added to Peter's sense of futility. "If I could only send him away to school, Mr. Hansen," he said. "But I can't. I don't even know where there is a school I could send him."

"No," said Mr. Hansen. "That is the trouble. I guess there are schools in Omaha, but I hear they cost a lot of money. Couldn't he go again this winter to the country school?"

"He has already said he will never go back there."

Peter didn't tell Mr. Hansen why. During the previous winter there had developed an open hostility between the boys under the leadership of Bert Dance and James Square against Alfred. It was due to the complete inability of these boys to appreciate or understand Alfred's interest in books. He on his part was too proud and superior in his attitude toward them. Every noon hour he sat at his desk reading books on history that the new teacher brought him from his home. The new teacher was a man who controlled the boys very well, while they were in the school, but he was not the type of person who could really develop a spirit of harmony among them.

He soon recognized Alfred's ability and gave him more attention than he showed to the rest of the pupils. He brought Alfred books, talked to him at recess, often kept him for ten or fifteen minutes after school to give him special help. Thus instead of bridging the old enmities that existed in the school he only gave them purpose and direction, helping to point them at Alfred. His generosity and interest so well meant only fanned the flame of hatred always smoldering in the hearts of the other boys against this particular one who seemed to be the teacher's favorite.

One day late in February the conflict broke out into an open fight. It was after school and Alfred was carrying a book home, wrapped in a newspaper. It was an illustrated copy of *Uncle Tom's Cabin* which he had been reading that day. After school, the teacher seeing how interested the boy was, said, "You may take it home for the night, if you like, Alfred."

"Oh, thank you, teacher," he had said, his voice almost choking with emotion over his kindness. "I'll wrap it in a newspaper so that it won't get soiled. I'll be awfully careful with it."

"I know you will. And you can have others to take home with you after you finish this one."

Alfred had never before in his life felt so proud. It was as though a new world had opened up before him. He did not even want his brothers to talk to him as they walked off the school yard together, because he wanted to hold his thoughts to himself in silence. He clutched the book under his arm, and thought of the wonderful evenings he would have after the chores were done.

About ten of the boys were standing in the road a short distance from the school house, but far enough away to be concealed by the thorn hedge from the school house windows. As the Grimsen boys approached James Square stepped up, and said, "What's the book under your arm, Alfred?" As he spoke he grabbed it away from Alfred who was taken completely off his guard. As Alfred reached for it, James threw it to Bert. Alfred rushed for it, but Bert threw it over his head back to James again. In the meantime the paper had been torn off. When Alfred turned too quickly for James to throw it back to Bert again, he threw it into a pool of snow and wet slush by the road side,

Alfred was beside himself with fury. He rushed at

James with all his strength and in a moment had him down on his back. Alfred pounded his face almost to a pulp before the other boys thought of interfering. Then they jumped into the fight. They rolled Alfred over on his side so that James got on the top and then Bert, who always managed to spare himself, kicked Alfred in the nose, tearing a long gash with the iron cleat he had nailed into the toe of his boot to save the leather from wearing out. When they saw Alfred suddenly cease struggling and lie quiet with the blood flowing all over his face, they all became frightened and ran away.

David and Hans had been helpless, crowded to one side. The whole affair lasted only a brief two minutes, so they could do nothing, not even run back to call the teacher. Only two minutes, but long enough to change the whole course of Alfred's life. When he finally got up from the road, bloody and wet, David handed him the book, which he had fished from the muddy slush by the road side. Alfred took one look and threw it back in the mud. "Leave it there," he said in a tone so savage that the boys could not refuse his command.

That was all he said. He did not curse the boys or rave at them as he had always done at other times when there had been trouble. He was silent during the long walk through the fields. When they reached the creek near home he stopped by a spring and washed his face free of all blood stains. It was badly swollen and the cut on his nose was deep and red. When he had finished washing himself he spoke for the first time. "How does it look now. Is the blood all gone?"

"Yes, Alfred, it's all gone," said David.

"Good. I am now completely through with school, and I want you kids to know that not one word is to be said at home about the book."

He spoke very quietly, and the boys knew he meant it.

When he entered the kitchen, and was met with the questions of his father and mother, he told them briefly how the boys had piled on him led by James Square, and then ended up with exactly the same words he had said to his brothers.

He never returned to Laurel Hope, nor did he say one word about *Uncle Tom's Cabin*. Whether the teacher knew what had happened or not no one ever discovered. David and Hans looked for the book the next day, but it was not to be found. Someone had picked it up and carried it away.

5

As the summer dragged on Peter for a time became almost friendly with the boys. He did little special things for them that year. At Easter time he had given each one of the boys the right to spend two dollars at the clothing store in Weeping Willow. Hans had been fearfully excited over that for the three oldest, to whom this special favor was granted, were to drive into town on Saturday night to make their purchases. Hans debated over what he should buy. He talked with his mother about it. It finally came down to a decision between a pair of shoes or a hat.

At last he decided on the hat. It was a black felt hat

with a narrow straight brim. It seemed to him as he sat on the wagon seat going out of town that night as though something wonderful had happened to him. He felt older, more important. Every time he leaned over the side of the wagon to spit, he put one hand on his hat. In order to win praises for his new hat, he would compliment David on the new shoes he was wearing, and he even remarked to Alfred about the shirt and necktie wrapped in a neat package and held in his lap.

Before they reached home the wind came up from the southeast. It developed into a dust storm after the first half-hour. Hans worried about his hat, and finally grew so tired holding it with his hand, that he decided to remove it and hold it in his lap. Just as he lifted it from his head a gust of wind tore it from his hand.

David and Hans spent a futile half-hour in searching in the dark for the lost hat, while Alfred stayed by the horses. "It's no use, Hans. You'll have to come over here and look for it tomorrow," said David.

Hans did not reply. He accepted the decision in silence. The next day which was Easter, he walked for hours over the plowed fields where his new hat had been carried by the wind the night before. He came home tired, hungry, and disappointed. All he said to his mother was "I should have bought shoes, but it's too late now to think of that."

Peter could not refrain from scolding Hans for being careless of his hat. "Why couldn't you hold on to it?" he said. But Hans didn't answer. Peter could never quite understand how to talk to his boys. He often forgot to make allowances for forces of nature when he dealt with them, and he never seemed to understand their problems.

Meta felt too sorry for Hans to refrain from interfering. "You ought to remember that anyone can lose a hat in a strong wind. Didn't you arrive in America bare-headed because you lost both of your hats at sea, not just one, but both of them? And the one was a stiff hat too, the like of which you have never had since you came to America."

Peter didn't reply. It seemed as though he had determined not to be so severe with the boys any more. But what Peter determined no one knew, nor was he able at all times to decide what his actions would be. There were too many forces in the world which for all Peter could tell, seemed to move in a dark, blundering, aimless fashion, but not so aimless as to miss him in passing.

One day that summer as he was cultivating corn, Hans brought him a letter along with the forenoon lunch. Peter saw it was from the old country, and his heart sank as he remembered that he had not written to his mother since Christmas. He opened the letter with nervous, clumsy fingers. The letter was from his brother and informed Peter that his mother was dead.

Only last year Peter promised himself that he would go home for a visit. That was while he counted the number of his hogs before they were born. Now it was too late. He sat on the beam of the cultivator with his head bowed in his hands, his lunch uneaten.

Hans was deeply impressed. "What is it, father," he asked, "Is it bad news again?"

"Yes, my son, it is. My mother is dead."

"Oh!" said Hans, and tried to imagine what it would be like to die over there in Denmark. "Don't you want to eat your lunch, father?"

"No, you can eat it, if you like, and then take the letter home to your mother."

He got up, put the lines around his back, and then as if he did not care to speak even to the horse, he set them in motion down the corn rows by slapping them with the reins.

After dinner he told the boys to unharness the horses. "We'll not work this afternoon," he said. He sat at the table with his head bowed upon his folded arms, as his sorrow carried him back home once more to the life there, and to that one experience which hung like a cloud over his life, and that had sent him away from his mother many years before. Now she was dead. Before long, if he should go back, he would have to visit his best loved friends at the graveyard. He would have to communicate with inscriptions on stone.

As he sat musing over the sad past, he heard his children planning to go swimming. The death of their grandmother was a fact, no doubt, but nothing more. Alfred was the only one who could remember her. His recollection of her was but a dim picture of a gray-haired, old lady. The half holiday just proclaimed was a reality that they could understand. Peter was shocked to hear their plans, and spoke up:

"No, boys, you can't go swimming today. Can't you understand why I am letting you out of work? Don't you know what it means to me to have my mother die? What if your mother should die?"

He then pictured for them in vivid language their sad plight if they should lose their mother, and he kept it up until the older boys felt embarrassed for him and the younger ones were in tears. And he kept them from swimming.

Yes, that was it, the remembered past. It came to steal away the pleasure of the present, when the present was not itself so filled with misery and struggle that not even the past with its ghosts of sorrow could make itself heard.

6

At last the corn-plowing was over again for another year. The cultivators were backed into the shade of a tree and the shovels were smeared with a heavy coat of axle grease. Peter was in good spirits. The corn looked fine, the cattle were feeding in the pasture where the blue grass had not yet shown signs of giving out. There had been ample rains so far. The wheat was turning yellow, giving the whole landscape a checker-board effect. Not a single thing had happened to interfere with the crops nor the cattle. Peter had fifty

fine hogs and not a sign of cholera anywhere in the
country. Even Meta's chickens seemed to be unmolested by the rats this year. There was peace and
quiet everywhere.

For Bounce it was the Indian Summer of life. She
was getting old and gray. If anyone removed her
pillow, a very special one that Meta had made for her,
from the corner, she would act very cross, as if she
might be imitating Peter when he lectured to the
family. Bounce had seen many things in this family,
and now as the summer days passed she seldom went
to the fields with the boys. She watched her son
Hobson follow the teams out of the yard, even at times
going as far as the road with them. There she
would stop, sit down and through half-closed eyes
watch them depart. Then as if to say "What's
the use of all this," she turned back to the house,
where she would give only one scratch at the door,
knowing that more effort was unnecessary. Meta
would be sure to hear her, and she always did. Sometimes Bounce would accept a little bite of second breakfast, but usually she just wagged her tail to show her
appreciation of Meta's offer, and then retired to her
corner. It was so good to rest now in old age. So much
had happened, so many tiresome, stormy, sad things
that it was best to just sleep through the days, perhaps dreaming of the past, but mostly just forgetting
that there was anything like a past. She had earned her
rest and not even Peter questioned her right to do
whatever she liked. If a hen strayed through the open

door into the kitchen, Meta would run to chase it out
before it could disturb Bounce's slumber, for if there
was anything that aroused Bounce's anger it was to see
some fool hen come into the kitchen as though it had
rights equal to human beings and dogs.

7

And now that cultivating was over Peter planned to
take the whole family to town. He had secretly decided
to buy Alfred a new suit of Sunday clothes. Perhaps
Peter had begun to see that he must try to do a little
more for Alfred than he had done in the past. It may
be that he thought Alfred would find better compan-
ions in Weeping Willow, if he could dress more like
the other young men in town.

It was Saturday morning and the boys hurried with
the chores so that they could make an early start for
town. By nine o'clock they were all in the kitchen
finishing their coffee and a bite of lunch. Meta began
helping the little ones dress, while David and Hans
washed the dishes. Alfred sat by the kitchen table with
his chin propped on his right hand. He was silently
staring through the open door.

"You must hurry now, Alfred, we are almost
ready."

"I don't think I'll go."

Meta's heart sank. She did not know what Peter's
plans were, but ever since that terrible quarrel in the
spring, she thought Peter had planned to get Alfred

a new suit. She had counted on this day as the proper time to bring it up.

"Oh, Alfred, you must go along. You know, I believe you will get a new suit today. I am going to speak to him about it."

"I don't want a suit. Let him keep his money."

He had no sooner said this than he regretted it, for he could see how it hurt his mother. But now it was said. Meta somehow always made the children feel that she was on their side, but even so, or because they knew it was safe, they often tortured her with their bitterest reproaches against their father and against the hard life on the farm.

"He will be awfully mad if you don't go. Please spare me a scene today. I have endured too much to be able to stand it. Don't spoil this one day for me. You know I haven't been along to town for over nine months, and I just can't stand another scene."

"I can't go today, mother. I just can't."

His original plan to defy his mother had changed with her plea. So now he added, "I have an awful bellyache. I don't dare to go to town."

She knew this was not true, but for his sake and her own she accepted this as a way out.

As she busied herself with the final preparation, she wondered: "What can he be up to now. Can it be that he is going somewhere with his old friends? I must explain to Peter that he is sick."

"Alfred, you had better go up to bed, then, instead of sitting there."

He left for the upstairs room. Meta explained to Peter, who seemed a little worried, but decided that it was a good thing that someone could remain at home to keep an eye on the cattle and feed the pigs at noon. He went to the door on the stairway and shouted some instructions up to Alfred. Then all was in readiness and they drove away to town.

8

Meta was the first one into the house when they reached home. Her eyes searched the room as though she were expecting something unusual. In a moment she found it. Stuck in front of the mirror was a note. She opened it and hastily read: "I am leaving home. I am going harvesting in the Dakotas. I took six dollars. Alfred."

Nothing more. He didn't even say good-bye. He didn't say he would write.

Peter came in with the little children, leaving David and Hans to unhitch the team. Meta sat by the table crying, with the note in her hand. He rushed over and grabbed it. It was then his turn to read about how his eldest son had run away. So this is what they worked for, to have their children leave them just when they could be of help on the farm. Such ingratitude. As long as Peter could dwell on such thoughts, he was safe from sorrow. It was important now that he should think like that, for he must do something to keep down the terrible ache, longing, heartsickness, that ate into him. This was a personal sorrow and a public shame. He would have to tell people that he let him go. And he took only six dollars. There were ten more in the box, but these he had left.

That night Meta and Peter both lay quietly in bed, pretending sleep. Long after midnight, when Peter could keep up the pretense no longer, he said, "He could at least have taken all sixteen. My son alone somewhere with only six dollars."

And then he too wept for his son.

Now began the longest six weeks of his life. Every day he expected to have a letter from Alfred. When the first week had passed, he said, "Oh, it takes time to get settled. You'll see, Meta, there will be a letter tomorrow."

But there was no letter. He now went for the mail himself. It was a quarter of a mile to the rural delivery box, and formerly he always left that task to the boys.

Meta had long since ceased asking him about letters when he returned. Instead she would sometimes say, "I see you got *The Danish Pioneer* today. I am glad it came, for this issue is supposed to bring the concluding chapter to the story." He knew what such talk was for, but it was not always easy for him to enter into this game. Many times in the evenings he would walk back up to the mail box, trying to make himself believe that he might have overlooked a letter. He even took to getting there before the mailman came—waiting for him, and then saying, "Are you sure, now that this is all?"

"Can old Grimsen have lost his mind?" thought the mailman, as he drove away. "I never used to see him here, and now he comes every day. Well, I guess that is like Danes, so what to hell, Nellie, get down the road." With a crack of the whip he drove away.

Six long weeks passed, and at last the letter came. Alfred was well. He was with a big harvesting crew near Bismarck, North Dakota. But he said nothing about coming home, nor did he say where a letter would reach him. This was the bitterest of all. He did not ask how anyone at home was getting along—he didn't even seem to care for them enough to want to hear how they all were. And so the summer dragged itself to an end. The crops were fine, the prices were good, but in the hearts of Peter and Meta there was sorrow.

9

Alfred returned in time for corn shucking. He came home in rags, dirty as a tramp from riding in box cars. He had sent fifty dollars home, the rest of his wages he spent, losing his last cent in a poker game so that he did not have carfare home.

He came home again as restless and unsatisfied as he was when he went away, and more defiant. He now smoked cigarettes in his father's presence and Peter did not dare to object. His son was sixteen years old and a grown man. He was the eldest son of an immigrant farmer, the product of the struggle involved in tearing up the old roots and adjusting to the culture of a new land. A green hand with a walking lister makes crooked rows.

XI

"Now, FRANK, try to read this one clear through. There is no reason why you shouldn't be as well read as the rest of us."

"I know that, Hans, but I don't seem to care for reading."

"If you don't read, what will you ever amount to in life? See all those books," said Hans, pointing proudly. "There are four hundred and sixty-five, and David and I have read every one of them."

"Well, then I'm going to try this one. The picture looks good," said Frank.

"I don't see how you can help liking it. That is one of my first ones. I'll never forget when David read it to me down in the elder bushes by the creek. When he read the title: *Young Wild West and the Redskin Raiders, or Arietta's Leap for Life,* I knew that it would be good. You try it, and if there is anything you don't understand, just ask me, and I'll explain it to you."

Frank was lying in one bed and Hans in another. The two beds just filled the length of the room and were placed end to end. The heads of the beds were together so that one lamp, standing on a table pushed against the joining of the two beds, served as a light for both boys. Beside each of them, on the floor, stood a gallon pail, which served the double purpose of spittoon and chamber pot.

Here was the ecstasy and peace to which the older Grimsen boys fled night after night as the winter weather drove them indoors. No one ever came to this upstairs room to disturb them. Here many a plan for the next day or year or life in the future had been discussed. It was here that Hans and David had worked out the full details of a horseback trip to Oregon. They had elected to take with them only their most trusted friends, and in their company they had worked out the problems of the journey, such as the guarding of their camp at night, who would do scout duty, and who would be responsible for food. The dangers of Indian raids and white robber-bands had been thoroughly analyzed. Not one night would they ever go to sleep without at least two guards: one for the camp and one for the horses. It was decided that the guard should never stand by the fire, where he would be an easy mark for the enemy, but that he should be concealed in the bushes, at least ten feet from the circle of light cast by the camp fire.

"But what if some Indian should discover this ruse, and creep up on the guard and stab him in the back? He would bite the dust without a murmur. Then where would we be?" said David, whose experience as Carl Green, the detective, had made him an authority always deferred to in matters of crime. "Or what if he should go to sleep?"

"A guard never goes to sleep," said Hans.

It was not going to sleep that Hans feared; it was the awful darkness, with the forests infested with savages and outlaws. Many a time he had luxuriated in the keen-edged passion of this fear as he thought of the hours when he would stand guard, his trusty Colt's forty-four in his hand.

"A man could stand with his back against a tree," he thought as he now lay on his bed staring with inward-looking eyes at the page before him.

Dear to his heart was this dangerous trip to the West. Not only would all of them have horses, but also revolvers and rifles. The one thing that Hans yearned for more than anything else was a rifle. Almost all the boys in the neighborhood had a twenty-two, but not the Grimsen boys. Peter Grimsen had a horror of rifles, fearing that some accident would be the result if he allowed his boys to carry firearms. Every winter when the other boys walked over the corn fields with their shining guns, Hans and David, who were the two most anxious for guns, watched from a distance with aching hearts.

Hans shook himself, and glanced back to see if Frank was really reading. He was.

"That's good," thought Hans. And now he turned to his own story. He was in no hurry to begin it. These booklets, about nine inches by twelve, contained only from twenty-six to thirty-six double-column pages. One could easily be read in an evening, but in order to make them last, Hans never read more than half of one at a sitting.

He now contemplated with sensuous delight and

intense interest the varicolored picture on the front page. First he read the title with loving attention to every word: *The Bradys and the Lost Gold Mine; or Hot Work Among the Cowboys.* What detectives the Bradys were! Old and Young King Brady. Hans had followed their adventures in at least one hundred different stories. He mused over their many terrible experiences. Trapped in Chinese opium dives, lost in the deserts of the west, shot at in the dark, captured and rescued in "the nick of time." What men they were! How brave and noble, for they were always fighting for law and justice. No criminal ever escaped them. No crime was ever too baffling for them to solve. Their nobility rose above mere matters of money. Many a time they worked on cases for poor people and never charged a cent for their services.

The picture on this cover was delightful. It showed Old and Young King Brady in complete control of the situation. One villain, his horse shot from under him, was covered by Harry, Old King Brady sat on his horse with a pistol in each hand covering two desperadoes, each with guns in their hands, and each mounted on a horse.

Hans now read the inscription under the picture, which he knew from experience, with these tales, was a direct quotation from an actual part of the story:

Old King Brady levelled a brace of pistols at the two cowboys, while Harry bound the villain.

"Halt!" exclaimed the old detective. "This man is our prisoner!"

The cowboys paused, holding their revolvers ready for action.

"He's got them dead to rights, I think," said Hans to himself in a whisper so as not to disturb Frank.

At last he turned the cover and began to read:

Chapter I

The Old Tablet

At ten o'clock on the night of March 30, a well-dressed man with a gray beard was passing. . . .

Before long, Hans was lost in the reality of murder, mystery, clues, danger, trails that led to Mexico, and the Wild West and back again to the wicked and mysterious city of New York.

Here was the winter night life of the Grimsen boys. They read these five cent novels with an intensity that amounted almost to a passion. The school books never required half their time even in the school room, because the lessons were gaged to the mental level of the school as a whole. The library at the school contained about fifty books, most of them unfit for "real reading" as these boys thought.

"I'd sooner cut sunflowers than read Henty or Oliver Optic," said Hans. "Why do they have such crazy books anyway? When you see a book in a stiff binding you can be almost certain that it's no good."

"What about *Little Men*, by Louisa Alcott?" said David.

"Oh, I'll admit that's all right. But its kinda for kids after all. The only book in the whole school that's worth anything is *Uncle Tom's Cabin*, by Harriet Beecher Stowe."

"I kinda like *Poor but Proud*, by Oliver Optic."

"I didn't," said Hans. "You don't learn anything about life from such books. Anybody knows that it isn't true. No poor people ever get along like that. That kid should have tried to sell cobs in Weeping Willow, and he'd find out what's what."

"That's right enough. It's a kinda make-believe," said David.

"Yes. That's why I like these stories. You learn something. Now, take *The Indian Massacre; or Custer's Last Stand*, by An Old Scout, that teaches you about the Indians and the West. If you read enough of these stories you really find out what life is like."

It was no mere accident that the full title and author was given when mentioning a book. Hans and David made it a point to know the name of the author for every book they read. It was considered a grave weakness to misquote a title or give the author's name inaccurately. In many cases it was not difficult to remember the author's name for all of the Brady stories were by A New York Detective, and all of the Young Wild West stories were by An Old Scout, but in the *Fame and Fortune Series* there was a great variety of authors and these were all memorized. On winter evenings these titles and authors were often reviewed. First

David would read titles, while Hans named the authors. For each mistake he would receive an error mark. Then the order was reversed. In the end mistakes were totaled to see who had made the greatest number of errors.

This was a common pastime when there were no new books to read, for over half the time they could not get enough of them to satisfy their need. One order, if they were careful to skip an evening or two from time to time would not last more than a month. An order was twenty-four novels. The rule was to read only half of one each night, but there were times when it was impossible to stop until the end had been reached. Then, many times in the winter afternoons, the boys would have leisure for reading. Thus it was that on some days two whole novels would be read. When that happened Hans always sank to rest at night with a mixed feeling of exaltation over the magnificent stories and the sad, futile feeling that he was two whole stories nearer the end of the collection.

Hans was now deep in the story, *The Bradys and the Lost Gold Mine.* He was lying fully dressed on the bed, as was his custom. The lamp cast shadows into the corners of the room. A little warmth spread from the stovepipe which came up through the middle of the floor from the stove in the parlor below. There was an intense quietness, which helped to make him oblivious to the world outside the story.

Old and Young King Brady had been captured by the bloody outlaws. Hans turned the page and read,

Unarmed, and facing death, the detectives realized that it would. . . .

The door at the foot of the stairs opened with a noise that sounded as loud as a gunshot to Hans. He leaped to a sitting position, as did Frank also. Then came his father's voice up the stairs, "Hans, come down here."

"All right, but what do you want?"

"Come down here, and I'll tell you."

Hans wiped his mouth with his hands and went down to the kitchen.

"What is it?"

"I want you to go up to Mr. Hayden's place and borrow some tobacco for me."

"Mr. Hayden?" said Hans, as though he had never heard the name before. He was trying to gain time, for nothing that he could think of in the world was greater torture than to be sent on an errand alone at night. His fear of the dark was so great that even to go from the house to the barn late at night often left him pale and limp with terror.

"Yes, Mr. Hayden. Haven't you ever heard of him?" said his father with a touch of sarcasm. "Ask him to let me have a full pack if he can spare it."

Hans cast an appealing glance at David, who was soaking his feet in a dish pan full of water. But David did not respond although he knew that Hans wanted him to go along. At the table sat Alfred reading *The Danish Pioneer*. Pretending that he had not heard what was being said, he spoke up, "It says here, that four of the worst desperadoes and murderers that ever were in the State Penitentiary escaped yesterday. They are supposed to have headed in this direction. Farmers are warned to keep their barns and houses well locked."

Hans understood that this was a lie, and that his brother was teasing him. All the boys knew how frightened he was of the dark, and they usually took advantage of this to scare him when they could. His father did not seem to know it, or if he did, never gave any indication of it.

Meta spoke. "He's just trying to frighten you, Hans. Don't pay any attention to him, and the coffee will be ready when you come back. I have just taken a coffee cake out of the oven. You can have a good big piece."

She knew that he liked her coffee cake better than any other food he ever ate.

"Where is my cap?" said Hans, after he had put on his coat and mittens.

"Can't you keep track of your cap? You kids bother your mother to death with looking for your caps. Now, when I was a boy, if I didn't hang my cap in a fixed place every time I came into the house. . . ."

Hans had found his cap and hurried out the door, before his father had finished. These long discourses on his own virtues and moral perfections that Peter so often gave his children bored all of them. Hans was glad to escape that, but now he was alone in the night.

2

He started around the corner of the house and then paused. Should he go out the driveway and up the road, or should he cut through the corn field? If he went by the road he would have to pass that dark hole where his father's driveway turned on to the main road. This spot was filled with all sorts of gruesome fears for Hans. Even in the daytime there was something sinister about this place. It was really a ditch with steep banks—about twenty feet from the top to the bottom. In the bottom was an arched culvert which seemed more like some wild animal's den than a passage for water. Rank weeds, underbrush, and a few tall willows grew along this ditch, and on both sides of the public highway, extending also along the road into Peter Grimsen's farm yard. No matter how dark the night might be, it was always darker down by The Hole, as it was called by the boys. The Hole came to have a meaning. It was a symbol of evil and lonely places. Next to a graveyard it contained more aspects of the unreasoned terror of the world than any other spot familiar to their childhood experience. Every time they talked of ghosts, witches, holdups, murder, storms, and other terrifying experiences, they were extensions and elaborations of things that flourished around The Hole.

Once when Hans had been awakened from a deep sleep by a thunderstorm, he had watched the chain lightning strike into The Hole, as it seemed to him, at least ten times in succession, at one-minute intervals, and each time he had observed vast, amorphous shapes rise out of The Hole and spread themselves into the sky. Against the searing intensity of the darkness that smote the eye and heart of Hans after each blinding flash, these great, spreading, intangible and anomalous forms intruded with a clearness that almost paralyzed him with fear. It was as though they possessed two distinctly opposite characteristics at the same time. They were shapeless and indefinite, and also clearly marked out both in form and extent. Like shapeless giants driving over Thor's bridge to Valhalla, these ungainly forms, that both moved and stood still, seemed to engulf him. They seemed to be, without giving any trace of their creation, and they grew until they danced with wild, black, meaningless power, enveloping the house in a darkness more profound than that which followed a flash of lightning.

Hans watched them until his nerves could stand it no longer. He crept from the bed to the stairway, guiding his movements by the lightning flashes. He crept down the steps, through the kitchen. Each crash of thunder rattled the windows and doors, as if they were being torn from their casings. As he opened the stairway door into the kitchen, he saw the wild shapes again. They were pushing at the kitchen windows, reaching for him. They held him in their power, and filled him with an unnamable terror more horrible than the forked glare of the lightning and the prolonged crashing of the thunder. He stumbled through the kitchen on his way to the parlor door. It was then that he realized for the first time where he was, and what he was trying to do. He was being driven by a power inside himself that he could no more control than he could control the shapes that were pressing in upon him from the outside world; the shapes that were rising from The Hole. He discovered that he was heading for his mother's bed, that he wanted to crawl down under the covers by her side.

The sense of ineffable peace that would be his by her side filled him with a longing such as he had never known before. No sooner had he grasped the sense of what he was doing than there appeared to him with sickening quickness, the impossibility of carrying out his desire. He saw in his imagination his father lying there by his mother's side. He could not do as he had sometimes done when he was a little boy, up until he was eight years old, crawl into bed between them. It was at least four years since he had done that.

He opened the parlor door and went in, still moving in the direction of his mother's bedroom, which opened from the parlor, but knowing all the time that he would have to stop before he reached the door. By the next flash of lightning he saw a blanket hanging over the back of a chair. He seized it and spread it on the floor against the wall that separated the parlor from the bedroom; the wall against which his mother's bed was placed. He quietly settled down on this blanket with his back against the wall, and with renewed courage looked at the window to see if the shapes were still there. Yes, he could see them plainly enough, but somehow they were no longer quite so sinister. He began to observe them with less fear and more curiosity, and just as his curiosity began to dominate his fear, they vanished.

3

As Hans stood by the corner of the house trying to decide whether to cut through the corn field or go by the road, the old terrors of The Hole seemed to rise before him.

"I'll get the lantern," he said aloud, for there was real comfort in the sound of his own voice.

In the wash house by the kitchen there was a lantern. Carefully he opened the door so that he would not be heard. He found the lantern without difficulty, carried it to the back of the house and there lighted it.

"This is better. Now I can see where I'm going," he said.

He had not yet settled on the route he would take. Past The Hole would be best in one way, for the ground would be smooth and even underfoot, and it would thus be possible to make better time, so he started for the road. Before he had taken ten steps, and without a further word or argument with himself, he turned back, climbed through a barb-wire fence and headed into the corn field.

Here the frozen ground was very uneven, and the dead and tangled cornstalks often caught his feet, almost tripping him. Behind him they continued to rattle long after he had passed, for a bent, dry cornstalk will snap back into position with a sinister sound, especially when it is heard on a dark, frosty night.

Hans glanced at the sky. As near as he could tell it must be heavily clouded. There was a rather sharp wind blowing from the north.

"Perhaps it will snow. It is about time it was snowing," he said, and then he kept up a continual stream of talk about the snow, and how there might be good sleigh riding soon. All the time the night fears kept demanding their rights. He had traversed half the distance to Mr. Hayden's place, when the whole field seemed to shake with a violent sound that bore down upon Hans with a terrible swiftness. What it was he did not know, but in spite of his fear, he had presence of mind enough to know that his lantern made him a clear target for any foe that might be seeking his life.

He turned down the wick, and shook the lantern. It went out. Then he ran with all the wild furies of the world pursuing him. He ran until he reached the cross roads where Mr. Hayden's house stood far in among a dense grove of ash trees. He paused for a moment to listen. The rattling he had heard was no longer discernible.

"What could it have been? Perhaps it was a whirlwind," he thought. "Anyway I'm glad my lantern is out. I was a fool to bring it. Suppose there should be robbers around here, then wouldn't I be a pretty mark. Imagine Buffalo Bill carrying a lantern."

This was all very well, but he also knew that Buffalo Bill carried a Colt's 44 on each hip in addition to his trusty bowie knife.

Before Hans now lay the most dangerous part of his journey. Not twenty feet from the road and directly opposite the driveway that led to Mr. Hayden's place, stood a vacant two-story house. The fact that it was near Mr. Hayden's house gave Hans little comfort, for it was on the side of the road opposite to Hayden's, and also Mr. Hayden's lay at least a hundred yards back and was completely concealed from the road by the heavy grove. The only way he could get to his destination was by passing the deserted house.

This house was one of his greatest fears whether by day or night. Many a dramatic episode had been enacted in and around its premises. It had been inhabited up until two years ago by an eccentric old bachelor named Harrison Farmer. He was known to be a miser. He was old, filthy in his habits, half blind, and yet he was worth over a hundred thousand dollars.

Hans and his brothers used to go up to his place to visit him, for in spite of his miserly habits of life, he would always speak kindly to the boys. He was a friendly old man to all who knew him, but he would groan with despair if he was ever forced to pay anyone for work that was done for him around his place; work that he could not do himself because of his failing eyesight.

As Hans dragged himself warily along the road, he remembered the grim details of the old miser's end.

Hans' brother Alfred, who often spent long evenings at Mr. Hayden's reading his books and magazines, also called on Mr. Farmer once in a while. This old miser interested him. It was whispered about that he was a Mason, and that once when a lawyer had tried to swindle Mr. Farmer out of a large sum of money the Masons had sent the lawyer a warning. One morning when the lawyer opened his front door he had found a bloody dagger driven through a note and deep into the panel of the door. On the top of the note was a skull and cross bones, on the bottom was the Masonic Emblem. The note read:

Next time through your heart.

Alfred was interested in him, and always, no matter how late it was, he would glance at Mr. Farmer's windows when he passed the house on his way home from Hayden's place. There would always be a dim lamp burning in one of the upstairs windows.

It was near Christmas time two years ago, and Hans recalled it well, when Alfred suspected that something was wrong at Mr. Farmer's. He had seen nothing of him either night or day for almost a week. Since he was passing by he would go down to the barn and see if the old man's horse was in the stable.

When the horse saw him, it began to paw and scrape as if it would tear the barn down. Its manger was without a blade of hay, and even the bedding straw had been eaten off the floor as far back as the horse's tie rope would permit him to reach. Alfred gave the horse some hay and then went up to the house and knocked on the door. No one answered.

It was bitterly cold, and now he feared that the old man was sick. He hurried over to Mr. Hayden from whom he got a ladder. Accompanied by Mr. Hayden, Alfred returned, placed the ladder to the window he knew to be the miser's bedroom, and climbed up. Through the window he could see him lying there in the bed. Since pounding on the window brought no response, Alfred forced it open, and crawled in.

There lay Mr. Farmer dead; frozen as stiff as an icicle. His last droolings were frozen into his long beard, making an ice bridge from the bed covering to his swollen and frozen tongue, which seemed to have forced his mouth open revealing his toothless gums. Beside him, on a chair, stood an empty coffee-pot, and a half loaf of frozen bread. When they drew back the covers, they found his body completely surrounded by frozen potatoes. There were over a hundred pounds of them in his bed. It was learned later that he always kept his potatoes in bed, since it was the only place he could keep them from freezing.

Hans did not believe in ghosts. No, not at all, but there was something about this old house that was not pleasant. In spite of the dark, the eyeless windows stared at him. He himself was responsible for the fact that all the window panes were broken out, and that in itself was not a pleasant thought, for his father had suspected him of doing it. When he asked Hans about it, Hans denied it. His father must have had better evidence than Hans ever knew of, for he kept on trying to get Hans to admit his guilt, until finally he said to his son, "You are a liar. You lie to your father in addition to being guilty of doing something that you know is wrong."

That had caused no little disturbance to his conscience. He had not exactly meant to get involved like that, but his father had forced him to do it. "After all," he reasoned, "It was my father's own fault that I lied."

He gripped the unlit lantern in his hand, and tense in every nerve he walked past the house, looking straight before him, and trying harder than he had ever tried before to think of something pleasant. He tried to recall a poem, but the only thing that would come to his mind was a brief snatch from a Danish poem:

> *Hans Liv var fuldt af Sten,*
> *men paa hans Grav—i Døden,*
> *man gav ham aldrig en.*

When he reached Mr. Hayden's driveway, he began running again, for now a new fear assailed him. What if Mr. Hayden should be in bed? He would be in bed, of that Hans felt certain. Surely Mr. Hayden would not stay up this late. And then he saw a light shining through the trees. With difficulty he stifled a sob of joy, as he slowed down to a walk in an effort to regain his breath before he reached the door.

Mr. Hayden came to the door in response to his knock.

"Hello, Hans, come in."

"Hello, Mr. Hayden. Dad wanted to know if you would lend him a package of tobacco."

"Yes, of course I will. Won't you sit down?"

"No, I guess not," said Hans. "You see, I have to hurry home again."

Mr. Hayden went to a cupboard by the wall from which he produced a package of Granger's Twist. This he handed to Hans. He seemed to realize that Hans had been scared for he said, "Why didn't one of your brothers come with you? You were scared, weren't you?"

"Well, maybe a little bit."

"Your lantern blew out, I see. Shall I light it for you?"

"Yes," said Hans, for he did not want to explain why he was carrying an unlighted lantern. He wondered why he had not thought of leaving it on the path before he reached the door.

With the lantern newly lighted, the tobacco securely placed in his duck-coat pocket, he was ready to leave. As Mr. Hayden opened the door, he said, "Here, take this."

"Thank you," said Hans.

By the light of his lantern he looked at the coin that Mr. Hayden had given him.

"Twenty-five cents. Now what do you know about that? Jesus, if this won't make them look! Twenty-five and the seventy we already have. Ninety-five cents. Only another nickel and we can send an order. Jesus, what a night!"

Talking steadily, he tried vainly to keep his sense of

ecstasy alive until he could pass the old house again. One dollar would mean a new order of twenty-four books.

He only had another thirty yards to go before he passed the house. Up to this point he had kept his eyes fixed with terrible intensity on the flame in his lantern, and he had intended to keep them right there too, until he was well past the house. But he failed. The moaning of the wind caused him to look up.

"God, a light." And he sank to his knees in the road with just strength enough to extinguish his lantern. He looked again. The light was gone. It had been in the room where Mr. Farmer died. Hans saw his chance. If he ran, he could get past the house before the man, who had no doubt seen Hans' lantern could get down the stairs around the house and out onto the road.

Acting on this reasoning, he dropped the lantern and ran for his life. He felt sure that he was being followed, but this only increased his speed. When he reached the cross roads, he did not hesitate a moment, but darted under the fence and into the cornfield again. The noises he had heard there on his former trip were as nothing to the reality of the danger that lay behind him. Nor would he for anything in the world chance going by The Hole.

When he was well into the field, he stopped to listen, crouching between the rows. All was silent.

"I wonder if I really saw a light," he whispered, and then because he did not want to minimize the danger, he added, "Yes, I know I did. And I left the lantern, too. Well, I can get it tomorrow and no one will know about that, unless the globe is broken. Then there'll be hell to pay. Well, I'll have to get it back in the wash room without anyone seeing me."

He now walked on without a backward glance. It seemed as though the fear had left him proud of his adventures. What if he had been afraid? He had gone through with it, hadn't he? "A coward would have turned back," he said aloud. "I don't turn back. Never. I'm scared all right, but by God I don't turn back."

Now he saw the light shining through the kitchen window of his home. It was almost as though he were already in the house. When he reached the door and walked in he was as calm as though he had been on an errand in the middle of the day. There was only one thing that worried him. Would he be scolded for having been gone so long? It must be near midnight.

He opened the door and was startled to see the whole family, except the two youngest ones, sitting at the table and his mother pouring coffee. How could this be? He looked at the clock. It was half past nine.

"I'll bet he ran all the way," said Alfred, and added, "Didn't you see anything of the escaped convicts?"

"Hans is always quick on an errand," said his father in praise of Hans, as he received the tobacco.

Hans sat down. He couldn't understand this, but as yet he was not ready to speak. He looked at the clock again, and finally he said, trying to be casual, "Is that clock right, Mother?"

"Yes, I think so. Why do you ask?"

"Oh, I thought it was later, that's all."

"Now how *could* this be?" he kept thinking to himself. So he had been gone only a half-hour. "It can't be right. It just can't be. Yet, I guess it is."

"Why are you so quiet, son. Didn't Mr. Hayden treat you right, or what's the matter?"

"Oh, yes, he was fine. I must be tired."

"Well, drink your coffee and you'll feel better," said his mother.

4

In the room upstairs he revealed to David and Frank the great triumph, his money. This caused a real sensation, for the boys had estimated that it would take at least two weeks more to get the extra thirty cents needed to make a dollar. Now they only lacked a nickel, and they could easily get that next Saturday when they went to town. Thus they could make out an order for twenty-four new books.

This was one of their greatest pleasures. The first problem was to decide whether the order should be sent to Street and Smith, or to Frank Tousey. This was always a question that needed a long and delightful discussion. David tended to favor the Street and Smith publications, but Hans always preferred Frank Tousey, for Frank Tousey published *Secret Service, Fame and Fortune* and *Wild West*. But he did not want the question settled without debate.

Many times this debate resulted in the preparation

of a complete order from the lists of each publisher, David making up the one from Street and Smith, Hans preparing the one from Frank Tousey's list. Then each title on each list would be read and argued over enthusiastically, and without any real conviction in the tone of the one who objected.

Seated at opposite sides of the table, they now began to work making out their list. Before long, they heard their folks go to bed. Alfred came upstairs and retired. Soon all was quiet in the house. They now talked in whispers and argued over titles. Frank Tousey was finally selected.

It was midnight before they had completed their task. Weary and contented they took the list with them to bed, for David was to read the order over to Hans once more, now that it was complete in all its details.

How good it was to settle into the soft feather tick which covered the straw mattress of their bed. Over them was another feather tick, heavier and thicker than the one under them. It seemed almost as if they sank out of sight. Hans twisted himself into a comfortable position with only his nose and eyes outside the tick.

"All right, David, begin."

David unfolded the letter and in a whisper began to read:

Dear Mr. Frank Tousey,
New York City.

Please send us the books on this list. We like your books better than any other we know of. Please send them as soon as you can. We are sending one dollar in stamps for the 24 books.

1. The Bradys and Silent Sam; or Tracking a Deaf and Dumb Gang.
2. The Bradys in China Town; or the Worst Crook of All.
3. Winning on Wall Street; or the Farm Boy Who Made Good.
4. Young Wild West at Dead Man's Gulch; or Arietta's Clever Ruse.
5. Young Wild West and the Lost. . . .

David paused to glance at Hans. He was asleep. The long day was over for him. It had ended on a note of supreme happiness. For just an instant David was angry with him for going to sleep, then he reached over and pulled the feather tick a little higher where it had sagged away from Hans' shoulder. He laid his letter on the table, blew out the light, and settled to sleep in his own private depression in the feather tick.

XII

THE SUN was rising into a clear sky as Hans came
quietly out of the kitchen door. He stood alone in the
dust and looked up over the hill at the sun. There to
the east his thought had been turned a thousand times
in what seemed to him a long, long life. He would
soon be twelve years old and in all the years of his
remembering he had so often looked toward the east,
toward the rising sun—or the full moon when it broke
in fire over the corn stalks on an autumn evening.
Toward the east his life had been oriented by his father
and mother. They had come from the east, from far,
far east over the great ocean, over from Denmark. He
had travelled often in his imagination over that first
hill, and the long level road, and then over two more
hills and then the curved road by the creek until he
reached the stone quarry. What lay beyond that he
did not know. From there on the whole trip to Denmark was shadowy, except that it was far. He could
remember Massachusetts, but it was to him only more
hills covered with trees. In his mind he crossed these
rapidly and then boarded the *Norge*. In twenty-one
days he could cross the Atlantic in the *Norge*. That's
how long it had taken him with his parents when they
came from Denmark. And once there it would not take

long to reach his grandmother's home. Her house was beautiful. It was made of bricks and there were colored stones in the walks that led to the house. There were flowers by the walks and his grandmother always had roses in a glass vase on her table. It was all like that there. He had seen pictures of all these things, and many, many times his mother had told him how nice it was in Denmark and how her mother was so very happy. Why Hans' mother so often cried when she told about how happy her mother was, Hans didn't know. Maybe that was why he wanted so badly to see her.

He sighed as he looked toward the barn. How beautifully quiet and fresh this world of dust and wind could be at five o'clock on a June morning. The grass and trees were heavy with jeweled dew. The young corn was just high enough to almost hide the ground from view. At the other end of the pasture almost a half a mile away the cattle were all lying down. Near them Peter Grimsen's four horses were all on their feet. Daisy was cropping the grass, while Barney was as usual pressing his breast against the barbed wire reaching for the grass on the other side of the fence. He always did that. It was the way of some horses to eat like that. Kitty was very close to Barney, but too wise to exert herself by trying to eat by reaching over the barbed wire.

Hans was not interested in Barney and Daisy, nor even Kitty. He was looking for Prince. It was thinking about Prince that had gotten him out of bed before any one else this Sunday morning. On Sunday everybody slept late. Even Meta didn't get up till six o'clock. Today Hans was up an hour earlier than his mother, because he was worried about Prince.

Alfred had come from the field yesterday afternoon at three o'clock. Prince had stopped half way down the field and refused to move. Alfred had lashed him again and again with the cruel whip that hung by a string from his right wrist. It was a long piece of baling wire tied to a short stick. The baling wire was long enough so that if skillfully swung it could hit the horse from his hind flank to his ears. But in spite of whippings that had raised welts along Prince's sides, he had refused to move. Alfred had been compelled to unhitch the team and bring it home.

2

Peter Grimsen knew what was wrong with Prince, and why the horse had now refused to work even though he had always been one of the most willing faithful horses Peter Grimsen owned. Prince had a fistula on his neck that for the last week had been swelling more and more every day. The strong horse liniment Peter purchased from Watkins' medicine man, which he rubbed on Prince's neck and shoulders every day had removed most of the hair, but the swelling continued. Peter said that the fistula must be opened, but that it would not do to open it until it had swelled to a head. What Peter hoped was that Prince would be able to work for another week, and by that time the corn would be cultivated the second time.

Yesterday Prince had given up. The pain in his neck had gotten to the place where the baling wire whip meant nothing to him in comparison with the pressure of the leather collar and the pull of the tugs. Prince had quit.

"Poor miserable horse," said Meta, as he stood by the water trough at the kitchen door trying to drink, but able to get only a mouthful at the time, because he could not bend his neck in the harness.

"Now, son, you better lead him to the barn, take off his harness, and then he'll drink."

"He'll drink now or stand thirsty in the barn, I can tell you that. I'll not take him out again. He was so stubborn that he would not even pull the cultivator after I took the shovels out of the ground. I had to unhitch in the middle of the field. He'll drink now or go thirsty."

Meta looked over to the corn fields where hot dry dust followed Peter's cultivator over the hill. Peter would now be alone until Prince's neck healed. She knew how Alfred felt. The dust blew around his feet, as he turned to lead the horses toward the barn. She called to him. "Oh, Alfred, I have the coffee almost ready. Come in as soon as you can."

"All right." His voice sounded sulky as if he were

still swearing at Prince. Meta went into the house. In
a few minutes she turned to the window and carefully
peeped out. Yes, sure enough, there was Alfred with
Prince at the trough. He was unharnessed and as he
drank with his mouth submerged till the nostrils were
almost covered, Alfred was bathing the swollen and
almost hairless neck with cold water. "Poor Prince,"
she said.

3

Prince's sickness loomed as a calamity to Hans, and
this explained why he had risen from his bed on Sunday
morning as early as he usually got up on a work day.
It was not that his affections for Prince were especially
aroused. He even felt angry with him. There seemed
to Hans to be a hundred vital problems associated with
and dependent upon Prince's fistula.

On the tenth day of June, which would be a week
from next Tuesday, he would be thirteen years old.
His mother had promised him a birthday party, and
also it had been arranged for over three weeks that on
Saturday, the seventh, Hans and Frank were to take
their mother to town. They were to have new clothes
and new shoes. Just the idea of taking his mother to
town was enough to get Hans excited. Had that been
his only worry he might still have been in bed, but the
trip to town was mostly for his benefit. He was not only
to have a birthday party, but he and David and Frank

were all to have new clothes, and new shoes. Thus the party and everything else seemed to depend upon the condition of Prince's neck.

Every boy in the family, except the baby knew all the plans for the farm, and they knew how their few moments for play depended upon the success of Peter Grimsen's program. So Hans knew that this trip to town was to come after the corn had been cultivated the second time. Between second time and laying by there was usually a week's respite for the horses, and even the boys did not work quite so hard. They sometimes got to stay in bed till six in the morning, because Meta would say she over-slept, or that she was not feeling well. There were even times when she would say to Peter, "Now, now, Peter, you better have your coffee in bed this morning, and we can talk a little before the boys get up." And then if Peter felt real good he would say, "All right, Meta, just for today we'll do that, just for today." At other times if Meta made a mistake about his mood, he would scold her and say, "Do you want to make our boys into lazy, good-for-nothing loafers? Are they to lie in bed while the morning-glories grow over the corn rows and choke out the young stalks? No, by God, get them up at the regular time. Get them up, I say."

But if Meta said that she had over-slept, Peter never scolded. He might get up, and refuse to take his morning coffee before going out to the barn, but he didn't say anything to Meta. She knew what she could do, and she knew why Peter was often sad. There were so many things in this new land. Nine years, now they had been in America, and it was still the new land.

4

Hans had gotten up this morning to see how Prince was getting along. It was quite clear to Hans that if Prince should be unfit for field work next week, the cultivating would not be finished by Saturday, and that if it were unfinished, he would not get to go to town. Then there would be neither clothes nor shoes, and without new clothes and shoes he did not want a party. He would not invite anyone, much less Mildred and her brother. It was Mildred with the long yellow curls, whom he wanted at his party. If she would only come, he thought, he would get a chance to talk to her, and then she would fall in love with him. Some day they would have a farm of their own. And his mother could come to see them. Only Mildred was not Danish and he didn't believe she would ever speak Danish. That was something to think about. He would think about it some more on another day. Maybe they could go to Denmark for a visit sometime, and then she would just naturally speak Danish.

There was so much trouble for Hans this morning that he scarcely heard the chorus of birds that sang with the joy of summer. He reached the barn and was impelled to watch the mud swallows at work. How they fascinated him! They were builders who worked in mud. Even with mud a beautiful house could be made, if you only knew how. He counted the little mud houses plastered under the eves of the barn. There were sixteen of them, and they all fitted so perfectly into the corners where the rafters protruded.

Hans was bare-headed and barefooted. He wore a cotton shirt, the sleeves cut off at the elbows and a pair of blue overalls. He leaned against a fence post and stretched one arm along the barbed wire as he watched swallows busy at the little house doors. One came back from the creek with a big worm. For a moment she fluttered at the door of her home and then she went inside. "Can they have young ones there already?" he said. For a moment he hesitated and then resisted the temptation to climb up for a peek in at the little door. He must be on his way to the pasture.

He saw Prince standing all by himself. He wasn't eating, nor did he move or show any interest when Hans approached. This was enough to tell Hans that Prince's condition had not improved during the night. He stood like a horse of wood. His eyes were open but he did not seem to see Hans nor anything. "Damn, you, Prince. Damn, you, anyway," said Hans as he walked up to him filled with anger at him for being sick. He stood real close to him looking into his eyes, and then as if something else that was not his own will spoke through him he said, "Poor old Prince. Poor old Prince," and he raised his hand very slowly to touch the sore neck which was swelled to a lump as big as a small milk pail. The swelling bulged on the sides and the top of the neck. It was a greenish red near the top where the Watkin's liniment had burned off the hair. As he raised his hand slowly to feel of Prince's neck, he seemed to shrink up his body and lean away from Hans although he did not move his feet, nor had he even turned his head. It was as if his body highly sensitized by his painful infection could feel a movement which he could not see. Hans knew that Prince was asking for help, and that he did not move away because he believed that Hans would and could help him. Very gently Hans laid his hand on the swollen neck. It was as hard as a rock. He held his hand there until Prince's body began to tremble with pain, but still the horse held his position. "Poor, old Prince. I'll take you home and see what Dad can do."

He went on up the pasture where the cattle had now risen and were feeding on the rich blue grass. In his feet he felt the pleasant thrill of occasionally stepping from the cool, wet, dewdrenched grass onto places where the grass was flattened down, dry and warm from the body of the animal that had slept there through the night.

He rounded up the cattle and began driving them toward home, where the cows would soon have to be milked. When he got back to the place where Prince stood, he undid the short rope which was tied to the horse's halter and led him, slightly protesting, home to the barnyard. After he closed the gate on the cattle, he took Prince to the barn and tied him in his stall. He then went to the house where he had already seen the white smoke of the corncob fire rising from the chimney.

5

Hans was wiping the dishes for his mother, and they had been talking about the trip to town. "You can't tell anything about it, Hans. It might rain so that they can't work in the field, and then we could have Kitty and Daisy."

"Oh, mother, you know it won't rain. How could it? And why couldn't we go anyway? We could start early and be home by noon. Now, couldn't we do that?"

"No, your father wouldn't lose a half a day's work. He can't afford to do that just at this time. And then you know on your birthday you and David will be free from morning till night, except for the chores."

"Well, I won't have a party if I can't have new clothes and I don't see why we always have to work and work. Almost every day the Dance kids go clear down to Weeping Willow Creek to fish and swim, and we. . . ."

He was interrupted by his father's voice calling him from the yard. He ran to the door, and answered briefly, "What?"

"Bring me the scissors," said his father.

"Mother, where are the scissors?" said Hans.

"They're in the parlor, but what does he want them for?"

"I don't know."

Hans found the scissors and went out into the yard where he now saw that his father had tied Prince's halter-rope up real close to the trunk of a box elder tree. He had tied it so that the horse had only about four inches play in his rope. As Hans walked up Alfred came from the barn carrying a twitch in his hand. This stick, an inch square and about one foot long, had a small quarter-inch rope that was fixed in a loop on the end of it. This loop was about six inches in diameter and was now fastened to the horse's upper lip. Alfred then turned the stick winding the rope until it had tightened onto the horse's lip so firmly that it seemed to squeeze out all the blood.

"Now, Alfred," said his father, "that's tight enough, but if he tries to struggle turn it tighter and pull down on it. Then, watch his front feet, because he might try to strike you with them. I have tied his head so close to the tree that I don't believe he can raise up enough to permit him to strike you, but be careful and watch him."

"He won't do anything. Why, he seems so near dead that he can hardly move," said Alfred.

"I know that," said Peter, "but this is going to hurt so much that he might do something."

Peter then turned to Hans and took the scissors and waved Hans off to one side. He now brought an old box about two feet high and placed it alongside the horse. He mounted the box with the scissors in his right hand and looked down at the swollen neck. He then felt of it very gently and talked to the horse, "Poor Prince, I'll help you now. Just be quiet, and we'll soon have this over and you'll feel better. You're a good horse. Yes, that you are, Prince, a good horse, and you'll get a big feed of oats when all this is over." While he talked and while Hans wondered what the scissors were for, he suddenly saw that his father's right arm was raised high up over Prince's neck and that the scissors were opened so that the most pointed blade was held like a dagger in his father's hand. Hans screamed with fear, for he now thought that his father intended to kill the horse.

His scream came too late to interfere with his father's action, for even as Hans cried out the scissors descended with frightful force and were plunged to the hilt into Prince's swollen neck, and jerked out again as Peter leapt from the box and away from the horse. For a moment Prince seemed to sink to the ground, as though he would have dropped dead on the spot, but only for a moment. Then he screamed like some wild animal that had caught its foot in a trap. It was a sound the like of which Hans had never heard from a horse. It was wild, high, terrifying. It seemed to echo in Hans' ears as if it would tear his ear drums out. With that scream Prince became a mad furious animal. He reared back breaking the halter straps and tearing the twitch out of Alfred's hand. He now turned and ran through the yard screaming again as he had the first time. He ran shaking his head from side to side as though he wished to break it from his body, while as he ran an arched stream of yellow pus and blood spurted high in the air from the wound in his neck. He ran blindly first upsetting the water trough, and then running into the clothes-lines snapping them and scattering the few garments that hung on them into the dust. He ran into the wooden fence of the hog pen breaking the boards into splinters.

Peter was yelling at him like mad, and cursing Alfred for not holding him. It was no use trying to stop him. He was turned by the impact of the hog fence, but now ran in the direction of the barn with his head down, and still shaking it, he plunged against the side of the barn and fell over stunned.

Peter ran into the barn and brought out a rope which he fastened around the horse's neck right back of the ears, and then giving him a gentle kick in the belly made him stand up. Prince stood up still a little stunned and bleeding from a cut on the breast where he had hit the hog fence and another small wound on the forehead from his impact with the barn. From his neck blood and yellow pus no longer spurted, but it oozed and occasionally bubbled flowing in a sticky stream down the bald, hairless neck. The pain had eased enough so that the horse was again quiet.

Meta stood in the doorway where she had watched the whole operation. She now went quietly inside saying to herself, "pitiful, pitiful horse."

Peter led the horse up to the water trough by the kitchen door, which Alfred and Hans had again placed on its stand. Here they helped one another bathe the wounded neck with cold water. Prince now stood perfectly still and even seemed to say he was pleased and happy. Again he seemed to know that these people were his good friends, and that they had only hurt him because they had to.

After they had bathed the horse for some time, Hans said, "How long will it be before he can be harnessed again, Dad?"

"That I can't tell, son, but if this heals at all, it will take two weeks at least."

"Two weeks?" said Hans as if he were asking a question. He looked up at the sun now well toward noon. It was clear, burning hot. He looked out over the yard at the broken hog fence and beyond it to the corn field. "Thirty acres there, and forty acres across the creek. That's seventy acres," he thought to himself.

6

As the days passed Prince's neck grew better, but it was quite clear that he would not be in harness for a long time. Only one cultivator could now be used but it moved through the corn rows from four o'clock in the morning until eight in the evening. By changing one horse every three hours it was possible to keep the cultivator going steadily all day long, Peter and his son Alfred taking turns at the handles. Even so, Friday morning came with almost half of the biggest field uncultivated. Hans had almost given up hope. That forenoon he had asked his mother to let him go around to the various neighbors and tell them that he could not have a party.

"Now, you wait till tomorrow, Hans, because I want you to watch the baby this afternoon while I go visiting."

"Visiting," said Hans in astonishment. "Visiting, why where in all the world are you going?" This was the first time in Hans' life that his mother had ever proposed to go visiting on a week day and by herself.

"Yes, I am going over to see Mrs. Square. It's only about a mile and a half, and I can walk there very well. I have often wanted to visit Mrs. Square. I think she is a very nice woman."

Hans was too puzzled even to argue. What could this mean? Why, his mother never went visiting and beside that, Mrs. Square was not Danish. How could his mother visit her? "But, mother, I don't understand. How can you visit with Mrs. Square? She can't talk Danish."

"Don't I know that? Try to tell me something I don't know, you who talk so much."

Hans was sitting in the kitchen and it was the middle of the forenoon. He had come in from the field where he was cutting milkweeds to get the mid-forenoon lunch of sandwiches and coffee to carry to the others who were all in the fields working. He wrinkled his brow and looked at his mother. "Could anything be wrong with her?" he wondered. Visiting Mrs. Square. But she didn't like any of that family. It was Square's son who had started the fight with Alfred that time when he had been almost killed.

"Mother, are you lying to me?" said Hans, unconsciously getting a perfect imitation of the tone his mother had so often used when she asked him that question, and on very sound suspicions too. Hans heard the imitation of her voice and accent in his question, and his heart sank, for somehow he knew that she would say no, just as he always did, and that he would not believe her, just as she always seemed to know when it was useless to believe him.

"No, I am not lying," answered Meta as she turned to the stove to hide her smile, because now she was enjoying the situation much more than she had expected.

"Well, then how can you visit with Mrs. Square, when she can't speak Danish?"

"I'll speak English," said Meta.

"You! You'll speak English!"

"Yes. Why not? Don't you think I've learned some English in all these years listening to you kids around here? Now, the lunch is ready so you can run along. And don't tell your dad or anyone what I plan to do this afternoon, if you know what's good for you."

This Hans knew not to be a threat, but a promise that he and his mother would keep this secret together. "All right, mother, but when will you tell me what you are going for?"

"Oh, sometime. Now run along."

That noon as they sat at the dinner table Hans

watched his mother and puzzled over this visit of hers. Then he heard her say, "Peter, I want Hans to help me in the house this afternoon."

"In the house! Are we having company that you need him in the house?"

"No, but I want him anyway, and I want you to let David come home for the lunch, because Hans won't have time to carry it."

"What's the mattter? What are you going to do? You are not papering the house are you, that you need to keep him home from the field?"

"Just the same, he has to stay home this afternoon."

"All right then, but what is all this mystery? Do you know, Hans?"

"No," said Hans very quickly. It was never any trouble to lie to his father. He could do that as easily as he could tell the truth. Anyway, he didn't really know what it was all about.

Meta had her way, and at two that afternoon she left for her visit to Mrs. Square. Hans had thought that she might tell him why she was going, but she only said, "Good-bye, Hans, and remember to have the coffee ready for David at three o'clock, and keep Karl in the house after he wakes from his nap."

Hans watched from the window, and before long he could see her going up the hill under the hot afternoon sun. She rather enjoyed the unusual experience she was having, and had her destination been to the home of some real friend it would have been wholly delightful in spite of the dust and the terrific sun. She had hated the Square's ever since that awful winter night when Alfred had come home all bloody from the kick that one of the boys had given him in the face. She could never forget that, because he still had a scar on his nose which was shaped like a figure seven.

All this was of little moment now compared to the trial of speaking English well enough to make her request clear. She rehearsed the words she would use. For the last three days she had been rehearsing them, and in some cases very cleverly finding out what the words were that she wanted from the boys without letting them know what she was doing or what her intentions were. As she climbed the hill she began systematically first saying the word in Danish and then repeating it in English. She could not but feel proud of herself as she discovered how well she could say them all. "Why, if the boys would only speak English to me, it would not be long until I could do as well as an American. I might even learn to read. Who knows?"

7

At three o'clock David came home for the lunch which Hans had ready for him to carry back out to the field. They talked excitedly about their mother's visit, but could come to no conclusion. The only answer they could get was their mother wanted to invite the Square's children to Hans' birthday party, but that seemed so far-fetched that it was ridiculous. David left again, and Hans began to watch the road for his mother's return. He knew she could not be on her way back yet, but still he watched. The baby was very quiet. The house grew silent. The afternoon sun was blue white. The flies hummed against the window panes. A great silence seemed to engulf time. Hans looked at the clock to see if the pendulum was really swinging. A great yearning love for his mother possessed him. He would run to her and kiss her when she came home. He had often thought of that before, but he never did it. Today he would, though. Oh, if he could only do it now. What if something should have happened to her?

He went to the kitchen door and looked out over the fields to where his father was cultivating corn and the other boys were cutting weeds. It surprised him, when he saw that they were really there. They were almost a half-mile away, but they were there, sitting in the shadow cast by the horses. They were eating their lunch. Hans looked at them a long time as though he could scarcely believe his eyes. Somehow he felt as though something terrible had happened. He could feel the presence of some evil shadow haunting him. It was just his awful fears come over him again. He knew that and told himself so, talking aloud and looking over the fields to the place where his father and his brothers were having their afternoon lunch.

He had resolved that he would not look up the road again until the clock struck four, and now it was striking: one, two, three, four. With the last stroke he turned, rushed to the window, looked up the road, and, there, already halfway down the hill was his mother.

It seemed to him that never again would he see anything that could make him so happy. It was like a flash of pure inspiration when he realized that she would not have had coffee at the Squares, for the Americans never served afternoon coffee. He went to the kitchen and built up the fire. "There's one good thing about the summer," he said to himself. "The cobs are dry." He put some water in the tea-kettle and washed out the coffee-pot. The cobs blazed in the stove and before long he poured the boiling water into the coffee-pot where he had already placed the grounds. He rushed to the window, but his mother was no longer in sight. "She must be at the bend of the road," he said aloud. Back in the kitchen, he set two cups and saucers on the table, teaspoons, plain granulated sugar and one piece of loaf sugar on the saucer of his mother's cup. Now, the coffee boiled and filled the whole kitchen with its sweet fragrance. He cut two pieces of cake and placed them on a plate as he saw his mother come in the door.

Now was his chance to do what he said he would. Something failed in him. He turned and said, "I suppose you have had your coffee?"

Meta didn't answer. She took off her hat and walked over to the parlor where she saw Karl playing with some blocks on the floor. She came back to the kitchen. "No, I haven't had coffee, and never have I been so glad for anything in my life as to see that you had it ready for me." Hans remembered those words all his life. Perhaps they made up for many things he had not done for his mother.

When Hans tried to find out why his mother had made her afternoon visit, she still refused to tell him, but she seemed pleased and more mysterious about it than ever. She made veiled references to the party which increased Hans' curiosity, but gave him no hint as to what she really meant.

That evening after dinner the whole thing came out. His mother knew that the Squares were the only ones in the neighborhood who had a single buggy. She had gone to them, suppressing her pride, and made arrangements to borrow their shafts. Peter was not pleased, for he did not wish to be beholden to Mr. Square for anything, but under the circumstances there was nothing he could do. With the shafts attached to their own buggy, the family could go to town, for they could drive Kitty single, and there would still be two horses for the cultivator.

8

Saturday morning all was bustle and hurry. First the men must be gotten into the field and arrangements made for their forenoon lunch as well as their dinner. Then David had to hitch Kitty to the buggy, the shafts having been brought down the night before, the tongue removed, and the shafts attached. Meta had to help Karl and Frank into their clothes, and all the boys had to put on long stockings and shoes. The shoes were all polished. She had seen to that before she retired the previous night.

At nine o'clock they were ready to leave. Hans sat in the front seat with Frank, who was nine, by his side. In the back seat sat Meta with Karl. Karl was so excited over his trip that he wouldn't even talk. He was four years old and usually very talkative, but today he would not say a word. He just sat in the buggy admiring the well-starched ruffles of his blouse.

Peter came in from the field just before they left. Hans was afraid he would do that. He walked round the buggy, tinkered with the harness, and warned them to be careful in crossing the railroad track. Then he patted Kitty on the neck and told her that she was a fine, good horse.

"Now, Hans, don't make her run too much because this is a heavy load for one horse.

"Meta, be careful of what you buy. Don't spend too much money."

"No, Peter, we'll be careful of that," said Meta.

At last they were on their way. It was a beautiful summer morning. Each turn in the road seemed to reveal some new wonder of green trees, flowery meadows and waving fields of corn and wheat. Everywhere men and horses were at work in the fields. How grand it was to sit here in the open spring wagon and watch the people at work. It was an elegant day for Hans. He was the master and coachman as well. Whenever he passed some farm house he held the reins in one hand and lifted the buggy whip from the socket with the other. Not that he used it much. Kitty was only too willing to do her part without the use of a whip, and besides his mother would have scolded had he started using it on Kitty. Still he could hold it in his hand like a real coachman.

When they came to Oak Hill, a hill that was quite steep and a half-mile long Meta told Hans to stop. He wondered what she wanted, but she just told him to stop. When he had halted the wagon, she climbed out and said, "The load is too heavy for Kitty. I'll just walk up this hill."

Hans was filled with consternation and shame. He knew that Kitty could pull the load, and that his mother was needlessly concerned for the horse. Why would his mother always do such crazy things! "Mother, you mustn't do that. Why, this is no load for Kitty. Now get in again."

"No, I can easily walk this little distance. You just drive on."

"I won't do it. I'll just stop here till you get back in."

"You do as I tell you, Hans," said Meta, being very stern.

Hans was desperate. He didn't want his mother to walk up this long, steep hill, but most of all he didn't want to be seen driving the buggy with his mother walking by the side. Halfway up the hill was a farm house. He couldn't bear the humiliation of having the people there see his mother walking. "Mother, can't you see what a terrible shame it is for all of us to have you walking? It's a disgrace. It's a shame that we'll never live down." He was almost in tears.

Frank was even more excited, and begged his

mother to get back into the wagon, until his mother told him to keep still, or she would turn around and take them all back home again. And then to settle the argument she began walking.

Hans swore to himself, but before long he saw that he had no choice. He let his mother get a good start and then drove on slowly up the hill. When he passed the farm yard, he looked straight ahead. If anyone was watching this foolish performance, he at least would not give any notice that he was aware of it. In this case it was doubly difficult, because he knew that the people who lived in this house had timber squirrels in a huge screened cage in their yard, and he had counted on seeing them as he passed by. But he wouldn't look, not even a glance did he give in that direction.

At the top of the hill, Meta got into the wagon again after she had shaken the dust out of her dress and wiped her shoes. Hans was sulky. Only the baby talked, for he had been afraid that his mother was leaving them, and had cried part of the way up the hill.

Meta soon had them all in good spirits again. It was never possible to be sulky with her very long. She could bring up such interesting subjects that you just had to give in to her. Thus they had not gone far till she said, "I wonder if Clark and Day will have neckties for boys? I don't suppose they will, because it's only a men's store."

For a moment Hans hesitated. He saw it was a trap but what could he do? Frank was all ears, and to remain silent would be to invite Frank to answer. He shrugged his shoulders and said, "Of course they have neckties for boys. I've seen them."

"Do you think we should buy one for David?"

"Yes," said Hans his heart sinking a little, for he had expected one to be offered to him. Then all of his anger seemed suddenly to have melted away. All that burning inside stopped. "Mother, let's get a red one for David and one for Alfred too, and I would like a blue one—blue as blue can be. I would like one that was real blue. You know what I mean, not blue like new overalls, but blue like that pansy we ordered from the catalogue."

"Yes, that would be nice, Hans," said his mother as her thoughts drifted back for a moment to the previous summer when she and Hans had ordered flower seeds and planted them all around the house. They had fenced them off from the chickens too by using old scraps of boards. But not a single one had grown. No. Not a flower bloomed in their yard. Only dust there stirred by the scratching of the chickens and the hot summer winds. Not a single bloom. Only a black weather-beaten shanty of a house that had never had a coat of paint.

It was nice to come to town like this, and see the pretty houses, especially the banker's place. They said he was a nice man. In recent years he let Peter have all the money he wanted. Sometimes he charged him only eight per cent interest, but it was usually ten per cent. They passed his place now. The yard was almost a quarter of an acre and all in grass and flowers. There were cool vines growing on the side of the house and large elm trees on the lawn. The house was shining white with beautiful green shutters.

At last the shopping began in earnest. They bought flour, coffee, tobacco, rice, salt, and some few things that were really extravagant such as a can of salmon, three bananas, and five cents worth of red sugar to be used on the birthday cake. After this was over they went to the clothing store where the older boys got new pants, and also helped select a pair to be taken home to David. Meta also bought new shoes for them, and calico for new shirts and blouses and even some to be made into a dress for herself. And they got new neckties, but not the blue one that Hans wanted. There was one almost the color he wanted, but it was thirty-five cents. He got a green one instead which cost only twenty cents. When the groceries were loaded, John Hansen gave them each a stick of candy, and at last they were ready to start for home again.

First they drove to a little side street where there was a water trough at which Kitty had a good drink.

"Now, Hans, drive over the bridge to the south. I want to see Mrs. Larsen for just a minute."

"But I am hungry, mother. Couldn't we go home now? Or, couldn't we go to the *Banner Lunch?* They have every thing you can eat there for fifteen cents."

"Yes, we should eat at a restaurant just because we are in town," said his mother sarcastically. "What do you think your father would say if we told him we had eaten in town?"

Hans knew what his father would say, all right

enough. He hadn't expected his mother to agree to his proposal, but he thought maybe he could keep her from going over to Mrs. Larsen's. Hans didn't like Mrs. Larsen because she was so horrible to look at. She had been a pretty girl once, his mother said, but she had worked in a garment factory in the city and had been burned in a fire. That was why her face was so bad. And after the fire her husband had died and she had a child to care for. They would not take her back at the factory because, as the boss very gently explained, it would remind the others too much of the unfortunate accident that had cost so many lives. As Meta always said Mrs. Larsen was a very sweet woman; she never even blamed the boss. She knew it was the truth that her appearance would remind the other women of the fire.

"But why do you want to see her today, mother?"

"Because she is very poor and she has no milk or vegetables as we have on the farm. I have a small sack of potatoes for her and a quart of cream that I boiled yesterday so that it will stay sweet. It will give her cream for her coffee for a whole week."

After the delivery had been made and Mrs. Larsen had thanked Meta so many times that it seemed almost too much, they drove on again. Mrs. Larsen had wanted them all to come in for coffee, but Meta would not listen to this.

Soon they were out of town and on the homeward road once more. Karl had gone to sleep on his mother's lap. Frank and Hans again complained of hunger. It was terrible the way hunger could gnaw at their bellies.

Just when they thought they could never stand it till they reached home, Meta reached under the front seat and produced a basket. Here were sandwiches made with her own home-cured, smoked sausages, and after the sandwiches coffee cake and two bottles of coffee. The coffee was cold, but it had a wonderful flavor.

"I didn't know you had all this food, mother. When did you fix that?"

"Oh, I did that last night after you were in bed. It didn't take long. The coffee I made this morning and bottled it while you were hitching up."

"It's very good," said Frank. "May I have another?"

"Yes, it's good," said Hans, and then he suddenly got out what he had wanted to say sooner, but couldn't say until he had the right opportunity. "You spoke very good English in the store today." There, he had said it. It was a lie. He had been terribly ashamed of his mother's speech, so awfully ashamed, but now he had said it.

"That's good of you, Hans, but I am afraid my English is pretty bad."

"No, it ain't," said Frank taking his cue from Hans.

But Hans said no more. He shouted to Kitty to get along.

9

Tuesday morning everything was in readiness for the party. That is, everything was almost ready. Peter had gone to a neighbor's two miles away on the night before to get a cake of ice. This neighbor had a big ice cave and sold ice in town during the summer. All that was needed was an ice-cream freezer, for one of the big events of this day was to be real homemade ice-cream. John Solve who lived only two miles to the north had a freezer which had already been promised for the party. All that remained was for David and Hans to go for it, which they were to do as soon as the morning chores were over.

They were just begging their mother to let them wear their new shoes on this trip, while she was telling them that it would be much easier for them to walk barefooted, than to wear their shoes, when Peter Grimsen came in the door. It was easy to see that something had gone wrong.

"Now, what in the world is the matter?" said Meta, hoping by taking the initiative to forestall a serious scolding. After all this preparation she felt that they must have peace for today.

Peter Grimsen was not to be put off like that. Some demon seemed to drive him to use every great occasion for a moral discourse, and all without his asking the text had just been given him. "You ask, Meta, what is the matter. And well you may. We work and plan to do everything we can for our boys. We slave for them day and night, buy them new clothes and plan a party for them with ice-cream. Do you think, you ungrateful kids, that other parents do that? Yes, mother, we plan and slave for them and what do we get in return? Hans loses the hammer, and David forgets to slop the pigs. These are everyday occurrences. I might as well talk to a fence post as to talk to them. Everything I say goes in one ear and out the other. But I thought that this week it would have been different, that they would have shown some gratitude. And, now, what have they done?"

"Yes, for God's sake, Peter, what have they done? Tell me what they have done, for I can't believe it is so bad as you seem to think."

"So you are taking their part again. No wonder I can't get them to do things right when you always side in with them. Am I to slave my life away on these clay hills raising more sunflowers and cockleburs than I do corn without even bringing my boys up aware of their duty and responsibility? How long is this going to last, this struggle to teach them responsibility? By God, I had better go out and bury myself in a clay pit and let the hot winds that dry my corn cover me with dust than always endure this opposition."

He was thoroughly aroused, and on such occasions he grew not only dramatic, but downright ridiculous, to the mortification of his family and to his own shame after the storm had passed. The boys cringed in their chairs behind the table where they had retired at the first burst of anger. There they sat ashamed of their father, afraid of him, and pitying him too.

"Do you want to know what they have done? I'll tell you, for it's no use to tell them. They don't care what they do as long as they get all the new clothes and shoes their fancy calls for. Oh, no, why should they care about us? What have they done? Last Sunday when Prince broke the hog fence I told them to fix it. I told these two, sitting right here before us, to fix that fence. I gave them plenty of nails and there are certainly boards enough scattered all over the yard to fix ten times over the place that was broken. They couldn't even do that right. They were too all-fired lazy to pick up a few boards or drive in a few nails. They don't say to themselves as they should, 'Let us fix this even better than dad would expect us to.' Oh, no, they say, 'Let's get this done as soon as possible so we can play,' as though all we had to think about was play. What are the consequences? Both of the red sows have broken out. They are nowhere in the yard. God only knows where they have gone. And, now, I'll tell you sluggards what you can do. You can find those two sows and get them back in the pen and fix that fence right before you have a party today. Now, get out. Get out, I say and find the sows."

"But, Peter," said Meta, "you know. . . ."

"I don't know anything except that they'll find those sows and get them back in the pen or they won't have a party. Do you hear?"

The boys moved out the door quickly as if they thought they might have to dodge a box on the ears on their way out.

It was then nine o'clock in the morning and the party was to begin at two. Hans and David quickly worked out a plan whereby one was to follow the creek and the other the road and then they would meet down by Murphy's place which was about a mile and a half to the north. If they found the sows then they could get the ice-cream freezer at the same time.

Noon came and the boys had not returned. Peter came into the table gloomy and conscience-stricken. Meta stood by the stove.

"Come to the table and eat can't you, Meta?" said Peter.

"No, I'll wait till the boys come."

No more was said. Alfred and Karl ate their food in silence. Only Karl chattered a little about ice-cream without knowing what it was, only sensing that it was something good they were to have in the afternoon.

One o'clock came and still the boys had not returned.

Peter came back to the house. He walked into the kitchen as though he wished to say something, but when he saw Meta sitting by the table with her hands folded looking at the birthday cake that had bananas in the filling between the layers and red sugar on the top, he turned and walked out again.

At one-thirty the boys arrived, with the sows too, and carrying the ice-cream freezer between them. Their father helped them drive the hogs into the pen.

"Where did you find them?"

"Down there," said David pointing to the north. That was all he said. Hans did not speak.

They walked together up to the house, where their mother had their dinner on the table.

"Don't you think the cake is pretty?" she said. "You

must eat in a hurry now so that you can get dressed before your company comes."

"I wish they weren't coming," said David.

"Don't talk like that, David. You get something to eat and while you eat I'll fix some water for your feet. Then when you get your new shoes on you'll feel just fine."

They looked so tired and dirty from sweat and dust that Meta could hardly keep a catch from her voice. She was resolved that this was no time to admit defeat. This was no worse than many other situations had been in times past. She knew how to deal with trouble. That, at least was one thing America had taught her.

Before long she had their feet washed and their hands and faces cleaned. She hurried them into their new clothes all the time talking to them. She asked about John Solve. Had they seen him? And had they ever heard the story about how he jumped into the water trough one cold winter day when he was shelling corn at this very place? No? So they hadn't heard that? He was standing by the sheller when a large rat ran out from the crib with Hobson chasing it. The rat ran for John and just when Hobson was about to grab it, it ran up John Solve's pants' leg. He jumped about two feet into the air and yelled like an Indian war dancer in Buffalo Bill's Circus and then rushed for the water tank. With one jump he landed in the middle of that ice water, and he just sat there until he had drowned the rat.

This did the trick. Both of the boys laughed till

their sides ached, because they knew John Solve well enough to realize how funny he must have looked with his long pointed nose very like a rat's dripping with cold as he sat there squirming in terror while he waited for the rat to stop moving under him in the icy water.

10

Mildred didn't come, although she had been invited, and neither did her brother. They were the children of well-to-do farmers who owned their own land. Meta knew why they didn't come, but she did not tell Hans. Anyway Hans was rather glad, because as the hour approached for their expected arrival, he grew more and more convinced that he would not know what to do with Mildred. She was the only girl he had invited.

There were eight boys in all, and since they had all know one another in school, they had no difficulty in playing together. They played Two Old Cat and Pass Around most of the time. After that they played Squirrel, which was a game of their own invention. The whole point of this game was to see who could travel the greatest distance in the trees that grew along the creek without touching ground. It was somewhat hazardous for many times it meant climbing high enough in one tree to make it bend over until the "Squirrel" could catch hold of the branches of another.

Hans and David had not wanted to play this game because of their new clothes and shoes, but when the others sensed this they immediately taunted them for being "fraidy cats." The result was that David won the race two ways both for distance and speed, but not without tearing a great hole in one of his new stockings.

The great event of the afternoon came when they were all to help one another make the ice-cream. This was to take place under the tree by the north side of the house. Meta had the mixture all prepared according to a recipe given her by a woman who made it in town every Sunday.

The mixture was poured into the freezer, the ice packed and salted, and the turning commenced. Hans had the first turn at the handle since it was his party.

"When it begins to get stiff it will be hard to turn the handle and then you will know it is almost done," said his mother, "and you must keep it going all the time."

"Can't your mother talk anything but that foreign language?" said one of the boys to Hans.

Hans blushed feeling the insult that was implied and answered, "Sure she can."

"Then why doesn't she?"

"Because she doesn't want to."

"Oh, I bet that's a lie," said another.

"Sure it's a lie," said a third. "My dad says none of these people can talk American, and that they don't want to."

"Who told him so much?" said David now coming into the argument and thoroughly angry. "You tell your dad that he's a damn liar."

"What? My dad a liar? Well, I can tell you something else too, and that is that your dad can't vote. That he ain't even an American. He's just a damn foreigner, that's what he is."

David was always a boy who was quick to fight. He didn't wait for another word. This boy had hit on the worst possible subject, the one about which the Grimsen boys were too sensitive. In a moment the two boys were rolling in the dust. The others yelled and cheered while Hans looked on in consternation. The two boys on the ground were now covered with dirt. David's new shirt was torn almost completely off and his nose was bleeding. His guest of a few minutes before was equally dirty and bleeding from a cut on the mouth, when Meta attracted by the noise arrived on the scene to stop the fight.

The boys stood up panting, while Meta scolded David.

"See, she can't talk American," shouted the boy who had been fighting with David, and then he added, "I am going home. Who goes with me?" Three others who were his near neighbors left with him, while Meta looked on. She made one attempt to stop them saying, "Now, now, go not," and then said no more. To Hans she said, "Keep on turning the freezer."

They turned and turned for over an hour packing in ice and salt, but the ice-cream would not whip up and freeze. This may have been due to the short period that it stood still while the fight was going on, or it may have been due to some other cause. The fact had finally to be admitted that it wouldn't freeze. However, it was fairly thick, at least so that it could be dished on the plates and eaten along with the cake. But there was no joy in it. David, after he washed his face went up-stairs to his room and refused to have anything more to do with the party, and all the others felt nervous, ill at ease and some of them ashamed of what had happened. As soon as they had finished with their cake they said good-bye and left for home.

Hans and his mother were alone in the kitchen. "Why did you spoil everything, Hans? Why did you do it?"

"It wasn't my fault, nor David's. That Bramwell kid said that you couldn't talk English, he said American, and that my dad couldn't vote, and then David called him a dirty liar. That's how it started."

"But you shouldn't fight with your guests. That's a terrible thing to do."

"I know it, but when they lie about you and about dad, then what should we do?"

"Hans, I don't know, because you know they didn't lie, for your dad can't vote and I can't really speak English. But it wasn't nice of them to say it to you on your birthday."

"Oh, you can too speak English," said Hans firmly. He did not mention the vote, because he was not just sure what that meant.

"All right, Hans, we won't say anything about it to your father. You had better tell David to come down for some cake. Then change your clothes as quickly as you can for it is time to go for the cows and to start the chores."

"But I'm so tired, mother. Can't I rest a bit?"

"No. Your father wouldn't like it if you were late getting the cows home. There can be no rest in this house till the day's work is done."

XIII

THE BOYS soon forgot the birthday party. Life moved
too rapidly for them to dwell long on the unpleasant
memories of that day. There were too many sunflowers
to cut and morning-glories to pull to leave much time
for brooding over an inward bruise. Life demands a
vigorous action to compensate for the dark shadows
cast by the brooding images of the mind. This was a
truth that all the Grimsen family knew in practice if
not in theory. Could they have paused and evaluated
life by any sane standard of decent living and social
well-being, they would have given up in complete despair, as would also hundreds of their fellow toilers on
the land. They lived in the midst of untold wealth
measured in the terms of food, yet each time Peter
Grimsen got ready to go to town he quarrelled with
his wife over the length of the grocery list. He knew
better than any one else how well Meta planned and
how carefully she refrained from ordering anything
that suggested extravagance. It was not with her he
quarrelled; it was with a power outside himself which
he could not get at, could not understand, so in despera-
tion he laid the blame on Meta. The time had not yet
come when an immigrant farmer could understand
why he could produce two thousand bushels of wheat

and corn and still not afford proper food and clothing for his wife and five children.

By hard work from day to day and month after month it was possible to give a certain concrete meaning to the meaningless. The cows produced calves, the sows pigs, the corn grew, the dry winds brought fear and suffering. The rains came to revive life.

The wheat harvest was upon them requiring even longer hours of work. After the dew fell in the evening the binder could not be operated even if the horses had been able to endure a longer shift. After the evening meal while the horses rested in the pasture, Peter Grimsen and his sons worked in the field shocking the wheat that had been cut during the day. It was after midnight before they finished their task and got home to bed. At four o'clock the next morning they were beginning again the work of the new day.

There was no time to brood over children's quarrels this summer. The wheat yield per acre was the best that Peter Grimsen had ever produced, and he had more acres in wheat this year than ever. In addition to his quarter section he had rented an additional eighty from a neighbor, a young widow woman by the name of Hilda Schneidermann. Thus he had thirty acres of wheat on his own place and thirty acres on the eighty. Sixty acres of wheat, and it looked as though it would go thirty-five bushels to the acre. That would be at least two thousand bushels of wheat and the price was around forty-five cents a bushel. He might get nine hundred dollars for his wheat. If he did, that would almost pay his rent on both places and leave his corn crop clear.

There was no time for the pale cast of thought to disturb the mind these days. With the harvesting came the need for extra help at threshing which meant also more work for Meta. In that furnace of a kitchen that baked day after day in the blazing glare of the summer sun she cooked and scrubbed and washed for her large family. It seemed harder for her this summer than ever before. That birthday party had meant more to her than it did to Hans. She was like the fledgling bird that falls when it tries to fly too soon. For a brief time she had seen herself as emerging from the narrow confines of her purely Danish culture into the new life of America. She had almost made herself believe that she could speak English and through new contacts forget the eternal ache in her heart which drew her back to the old country.

2

Meta had been hurt more than she even dared to admit to herself. To her also the heavy work of that summer was a buckler and shield for the vulnerable wings of thought. There were other things too. She was pregnant again. Once again she was living in a great hope. Ever since her first-born son seventeen years ago, she had hoped that the next child would be a girl, and once that hope had been fulfilled. That painful journey from Massachusetts to Nebraska had not seemed so bad, for she held against her breast the daughter she had longed for. Even the hut in which they lived sometimes seemed like a palace, when she saw Margaret's yellow curls brightening the room. Before the second winter was over Margaret had been taken away.

When Karl was born the fall after Margaret's death, she had again hoped for a daughter, only to find that she had another son. That was four years ago. Now she was pregnant again, and again the hope for a daughter was a beacon light to her spirit. One day that summer shortly after Hans' birthday, she had asked Peter to take her with him to town. He had objected, because he could not afford one cent for the things Meta always bought, such as calico for dresses and a kettle or two for the stove. Her answer was that she did not want to buy a single thing. He had then consented. When they reached Weeping Willow, she told him that she would just walk around for a bit, and meet him again in an hour. That hour she spent at Margaret's grave; where she first pulled the weeds that grew over it and made the place clean. She then wiped the dust and dirt from the little wooden marker which bore the inscription *Margaret 1898-1900*.

Meta was a strong woman who knew how to bear her burdens without tears. "How nice it looks now," she thought as she viewed the clean ground in the midst of all the weeds that covered this end of the graveyard. She now produced a piece of paper from the pocket of her coat, opened it out and knelt before the marker on the grave. On this piece of paper she had copied a passage from the Bible which she now read aloud. She could not bring her Bible with her because it was so large that Peter would have noticed it, and this journey of hers had been a secret between her and the God she trusted. When she had finished her reading she bowed her head and in soft clear tones that seemed to blend with the singing of the birds and the soft air of summer, she asked God to make the life that moved in her be a girl. She told God that she did not complain, and in words full of all the ache and desolation of her Nebraska home, she asked God for another daughter. She ended as simply as she had begun, saying, "Thanks, God, for listening to me."

When she turned from the grave she walked a few steps and then looked back. There was only a bare patch of soil and a wooden marker. A few steps farther and she was in the fine part of the cemetery. Here the grass was green and well watered. She paused at one grave which was nicely made. It was heaped with flowers and at its head was a granite tombstone with a carved spray of flowers over a cradle telling Meta, who could not read the English, that this was also the grave of a child. She stooped and touched the flowers with her hand. And then she turned away and cried with heart-breaking sobs. She had not wanted to cry. She was ashamed. But she had cried, and she had also said, as she walked away, "Even our dead must lie in the dirt, and without flowers."

3

Peter Grimsen was more difficult than ever to get along with this summer. The whole affair of the birthday party had finally been told him. The quarrel and the miserable end to the party did not ease his conscience any for his behavior to the boys. It made him realize how little they understood him or even cared for him. He brooded over their well-being and wished only to make good men of them, but instead he seemed to succeed only in arousing their dislike if not open hatred. His eldest son had already rebelled, and Peter suspected him of keeping bad company, although he did not really know how bad that company was.

More and more he felt that Meta was turning against him and joining his sons in their opposition. He often accused her of doing so when he was angry, but at other times he did not really believe this to be true. More and more he felt that he was standing alone in a strange land. He did not talk to Meta about his problems as often as he had done in those first years in Nebraska. Somehow he had come to feel that his problems were his alone. To talk to Meta always seemed to bring up the question of Denmark, and while she never said that they should sell out and return, he felt that if he were to do for her the one thing that would make her supremely happy, it would be to go back to the old country. This he was not yet ready to do. The spaciousness of his fields appealed to the love for land which was his most deeply rooted social heritage. The long corn rows stirred his blood and warmed his heart. There was scope for action here. The possibilities for the future in this new country fired his imagination. There was a challenge in this land that appealed to his courage as well as his industry.

Each of these elements in his situation was haunted by its own peculiar specter of evil. Peter Grimsen knew these shadows of ill omen as well as he knew the brighter forces that urged him on. He saw how he was failing to win either the love or the loyalty of his sons. He feared he was losing that close feeling of companionship with Meta which had at one time made even the greatest hardships bearable.

He had felt the deep insult of the birthday party. It made him realize that among the American farmers he was not a neighbor, but a foreigner. This then was also to be added to his burdens, as if nature did not supply enough troubles for him. Still nature was not so bad. If she were fierce and brutal one year, she sometimes made ample restitution the next. Not so the system under which he held his land and bought his tools, clothing and food. It was far more inexorable than nature. No matter what happened to his crops or his family, the rent for the land and the interest on his loans for tools and equipment never ceased. The rich harvest that seemed to be promised this summer would leave him little profit after he met the loans at the bank, and the rent to the landlord.

4

To counteract these elements of despair, a new interest had come into Peter Grimsen's life this year. It was something that increased his hope and made him feel more at home in America, in spite of all his troubles. It also gave him moments when he sensed a foreboding of evil, but these brief experiences he had so far successfully suppressed.

There were two separate aspects to this new interest for Peter. During the previous winter he had heard that a widow woman, a German, who lived about a mile away was offering for rent eighty acres of her land. This had immediately interested him, for now that Alfred was seventeen and David fifteen, Peter felt that he could even handle more land.

Acting upon the information he had gotten, he went to see the widow. Her name was Hilda Schneidermann. Peter had often seen her in the fields, for she worked like a man. She listed her corn, cultivated it, and shucked it in the fall. The only thing she did not do was to exchange help with the other farmers in threshing time and at corn shelling, or rather she employed a man to carry out her part of the exchange work. Otherwise there was no aspect of farm life that she did not handle by herself in its entirety. There were all sorts of stories afloat in the community about the things she had done and the things she hadn't. Some were good and some bad, but most people took these tales for the fun that was in them, since none of them could be proved.

She was not known to associate with anyone socially. She led a lonely life. People who went to her place at threshing time, and were given meals in her house said that it was as neat and clean as the white paint on the outside. Six years before this spring she had come from the southern part of the state with enough cash money to buy her quarter section outright. It was rumored that her husband had been a business man, and that her money had come from his life insurance. Whatever the truth was she kept it to herself. She did not speak good English nor did she seek the company of other women in the neighborhood, which accounted for both the stories and the mystery that surrounded her.

It was a clear cold day in January when Peter Grimsen went to see the German widow. He could not help feeling a little nervous about this visit, for he had not said anything to Meta about it, nor had he ever spoken one word to Mrs. Schneidermann, nor even been near enough to her to know what she really looked like. He knew she was rather large, and he had heard stories about how big her feet were, so he had imagined her to be very middle-aged and commonplace. That she might be attractive had never entered his mind.

Thus what was his astonishment when in answer to

his knock at her door, he should see a woman who if
not beautiful was at least far from being commonplace.
She was rather tall, very straight, full chested and
slender at the waist. Her hair was yellow and beautifully coiled on the top of her head. Her face showed
the effect of long exposure to the Nebraska summers,
but this only seemed to enhance the full redness of her
lips and the smiling blue of her eyes. Most of all he
was charmed by the very rich deep voice in which she
said, "Good day, Mr. Grimsen. Won't you come in?"

Her home was warm, peaceful, and clean. There
was a quiet and a freshness here that was in a marked
contrast to his own home where the children were forever making noise, slamming doors, and tracking in
dirt. Meta's plain dresses, sometimes none too clean
did not compare very favorably with the neatly fitted
printed calico dress Mrs. Schneidermann was wearing
this bright winter morning. On the table there in the
kitchen where they now sat down to talk was a pure
white oilcloth cover, and white dishes filled the cupboard by the wall back of the table.

There did not seem to be a moment's embarrassment
over their difficulties with the language. Mrs. Schneidermann laughed at her own mistakes and soon Peter
was laughing too with more freedom and ease than he
had laughed for years. If they didn't succeed in one
way to make their meaning clear, they tried another.
They talked of the crops, of that dry year which had
been almost a complete failure and of the prospect for
the coming years. Peter told her the story of Paulsen

who had swindled him out of his corn, and how he had forced up the rent on the place which he now farmed.

Gradually they came around to the business which had occasioned this call. Peter finally said, "I heard you wanted to rent out an eighty."

"Yes, I think I do, but I am not sure."

"You should do it, though." Peter was a little surprised when he heard himself say that. He even had time in his thoughts to wonder what business it was of his what this woman did. Peter was a man who drove a hard bargain as long as it was honest and above board. He was an upright man and prided himself on that fact. Thus he was immediately aware that as far as good tactics are concerned, he had said more than was necessary.

"Yes, Mr. Grimsen, it is a little too much for me, but I have not yet entirely made up my mind. Did you want to pay cash rent or share rent?"

"I don't care much about that. If the share rent is not too high I would just as soon give shares."

They were both silent. Finally Mrs. Schneidermann looked at the clock. "Why, here it is one o'clock. You must have a bite to eat with me."

Peter was startled. "I did not know it was that late. No, I must go."

"No, you can't do that. I won't hear it. You are to stay. Just a minute I shall have food for you."

She was already standing, and as Peter started to rise she laid a hand on his shoulder and said, "No, you are to stay."

She made sausages and scrambled eggs. She opened a jar of peaches and made hot biscuits and coffee. It was two o'clock before they had finished eating, and then nothing would do but Peter should go with her to the yard to see her brood sows. She had eight fine ones, all bred for late February farrowing.

It was four o'clock when Peter got home.

"Where in the world have you been, Peter?" said Meta. "I sat here keeping your lunch warm till two o'clock."

"Oh, I was just walking around looking over the land, and then I got down to Mrs. Schneidermann's just when she was making dinner, so I had dinner there."

"But why were you down there?"

"I thought maybe I would rent an eighty from her this year."

To this Meta had no objection. She knew that Peter yearned for more land, and that with the boys growing up they could easily manage another eighty. "Did you get it then?"

Strangely enough, this question surprised Peter. He suddenly realized that he hadn't gotten it, that Mrs. Schneidermann had not stated any terms nor made any promises. "No," Peter answered. "Not yet. She is not sure that she will rent it."

5

Peter had to make three other trips on three consecutive weeks before he got the land. He had finally decided that the young widow was playing him for a sucker and that she would raise the rent to such a figure that there would be only hard work and no profit in this deal. He had come to this decision on his second visit for at that time when he had asked her for a definite statement, she had avoided giving an answer.

"I must know very soon," said Peter, "for it will not be long now till we can begin to cut stalks."

"If you will come next Monday, I will tell you," said Mrs. Schneidermann.

As Peter had thought of this, he had grown angry, for he believed that she was going to try to take advantage of him. Everyone tried that, and he was used to it, but in this case he felt a deep emotional reaction. He pondered over it during the week, and three different times he had decided that he would not even go down to see her. "Let her keep her god damn rotten land," he had said aloud to himself as he was doing the milking on Sunday night. "I'll not even go to see her." But that same night before he had gone to sleep he had changed his mind again and made his plans for going to her place in the morning.

"Don't promise too much rent," said Meta as Peter left the house about ten in the morning. He was wearing a clean pair of overalls.

"I'll see to that," said Peter.

Peter would not admit to himself that he cared especially for this extra land. As he walked down the road he figured that she would probably ask half the corn and two-fifths of the small grain. That's what many of the landlords were getting these days, and if he had to pay that much it would be all work with no gain. What would Meta say if he agreed to such a rent? But whenever he refused in his mind to pay this imagined rent, something went wrong inside him. He felt sick and disturbed.

These visits had come to mean more to him than he quite understood. With Mrs. Schneidermann he had talked about America. Her accent was very German because she had lived in a clannish German community at Berlin, Nebraska, and she had been fifteen years old when she came from Germany to this country with her parents. So she had never gone to the American schools, but she had learned to read and she had taken out citizenship papers. Thus in a way she became Peter's teacher. Through her he learned many things about America that he had not known before, and unconsciously he had begun for the first time to feel that he was a part of the new country.

"She must be a damn smart woman, the way she can read," he said to himself, as his mind wandered away from rent to thoughts about her. "But I will not pay half," he muttered stubbornly, as if to fortify himself against the attacks of an enemy.

How nice it was to sit here and have dinner with her. For two hours now they had talked, and nothing had been said about rent. This would have to end. Peter felt suddenly nervous and looked at the clock. "Now, what shall we say about the rent?" he said.

"Yes, I have decided that you can have the eighty. What rent do you think you should pay?" was her answer.

This surprised him. Was she trying to trap him, he wondered. "No. I can't say that. That is for you to say," and he wanted to add for safety sake, "and for me to refuse," but it stuck in his throat.

"You pay cash rent where you are, don't you?"

"Yes. I did pay four dollars an acre, but due to Paulsen's meddling, I am now paying four fifty."

"Would you rather rent for shares?"

"No, I don't think so."

"If you want the land you can have it, for a rent of three hundred and forty dollars, that's twenty-five cents less an acre than you pay on the home place, but there are about eight acres in pasture land. Is that fair?"

Peter was so excited and astonished he could hardly answer. His mind was filled with the things he wanted to say to himself before he could answer her. He wanted especially to tell himself what a fool he had been, and what a fine woman she was. This could wait, he thought to himself and answered, "Yes, that's good."

"All right then it is settled," she said.

"Do you wish any part of it in wheat or oats?"

"I'll leave that to you. I don't care much for spring wheat, but if you want to put some in oats that's good for the land, but you do as you like."

Thus it had been settled. When he asked if she wanted anything written in the way of a contract she said, "No. It is to be three hundred and forty dollars. That is enough."

6

And so it had been settled that winter day. The wheat had done even better than he had expected. He had bought a second-hand Deering binder that summer, so that he could cut his own grain, and that had cost him seventy-five dollars. Even so it looked as though he would end the year with most of his debts paid. If that should happen it would be the first year in this country that he had been free from debt.

In spite of the bright prospects for the crops, Peter grew more and more irritable and dissatisfied as the summer turned into autumn. Since that day when he had rented the land, he had not had another visit like the ones he remembered so clearly from the winter. Hilda, as he now always spoke of her to his family, and thought of her to himself, had at times seemed almost unfriendly to him. Then one day she had met him in the field and asked him to come down and cut her pigs. Peter was known to be very skillful at this operation, and did it for many of the neighbors, but peasant farmer though he was, it had shocked him to have her ask him to do it for her. He had, of course, agreed to do as she wished, and he had taken Alfred with him to hold the pigs. He did not expect her to help. In this he had not understood her. She was right on the job, and caught the pigs for them, while Alfred held them and Peter performed the operation. She had forty-eight pigs in all and twenty-seven of them were males.

As soon as he had finished, she asked him and his son

to come in for coffee. Peter had refused rather sharply. Since then, and that was in May, he had seen her only two times, once when he hauled a load of hay for her, which she had mowed back from the hayloft window for him, and once when he had hauled a load of fence posts for her.

October had come and the first frost had taken the rich green from the corn stalks. The fields were heavy with long ears in shucks that were turning yellow. The rich brown silk hung like fine, woman's hair at the ends of the ears. Everywhere the farmers now walked through their fields admiring the fine crop that was assured. Peter often drew his hand lovingly down the ears of corn and let the soft, brown silk flow through his hand.

One day as he was walking over on the widow's eighty, he suddenly felt that he must see Hilda. Just why he didn't know. He returned home and told Meta that the boys were to do the chores, and that if she would give him a bite to eat he would go over to Van Doren's and talk to him about paying for the binder he had bought from him last July.

He did go to Van Doren's and visited there for two hours, discovering to his surprise how friendly and nice this American was, and how interested he seemed to be in Peter's plans for the coming year.

When he left there it was already dark, but the east was aflame with the bursting fire of a full moon rising. On the crest of the hill two great cottonwoods spread their naked branches against the flame of the east. The grandeur and beauty of the night smote his heart with sadness, but also it fed a new longing within him. The moon rose and flooded the landscape with a soft and lovely beauty. The round fertile hills of eastern Nebraska, rich with the fruit of summer on their bosoms and bathed in the light of a full moon were exquisite in their appealing loveliness. For the first time the hills and valley, the moonlight and the fresh, crisp frosty air called to something deep in Peter's heart as if it urged him to love this land, to forget the old country, to become a part of a new world. The bitterness of the past hardship was forgotten. Nature, the sweet, bespangled prostitute, seducing man to love her at night and in the heat of day torturing him to the very limits of his endurance.

It was twelve o'clock when Peter came home. Meta was waiting by the kitchen stove. She looked tired and worn. Big again with child, and exhausted by a long summer, she did not look very happy or very attractive, although she had her hair fixed nicely tonight and she was wearing a clean dress.

"Where in the world have you been, Peter? I sent Hans over to Van Dorens' to tell you to come home, and they said you had left there at eight o'clock."

"What did you do that for?"

"Peter Nielsen and his wife came to see us. They were very disappointed because you were not home."

"Oh, they did. I am sorry. I went over to see Mrs. Schneidermann, to see about renting her place again for next year."

"Why so early about that? There is no hurry, is there?"

"No, I guess not."

"Did you get it then?"

"Well, I don't know. She is funny about that place." And with those words Peter had lied openly. There was no escaping himself this time. He had not even talked to her about renting her place, and now he had lied to Meta about it. There was no avoiding that. Could Meta see it he wondered. His conscience could. That much at least was clear.

He abruptly went to the wash stand, cleaned his hands, and then said, "Let's go to bed."

7

Peter began to look more and more toward the future in America. He went often to see Mr. Van Doren, and before long he felt a greater solidarity with his American neighbors. One day Mr. Van Doren said, "Why don't you take out citizenship papers?"

This came like a shock to Peter. He thought about it for many days. Did he really wish to renounce all allegiance to Denmark and become a citizen of the United States? In the back of his mind he had never given up the idea of some day returning to the old country. Like all emigrants he secretly treasured the hope that by some means which he did not understand, he would again be back home and a well-to-do farmer there. Should he become an American citizen? So many things seemed to depend upon this action.

He decided he would talk it over with Meta some day. He tried to make himself believe that she did not wish to return to the old country. During those first years when they had faced so many hardships, she had always refused when he suggested that they give up and go back home. But did she really mean what she had said?

The wheat crop paid all but eighty dollars of their entire rent. Peter had a hundred acres in corn, besides the extra cattle in the pastures and hay and oats for his stock. The corn would yield at least three thousand bushels and prices were a strong thirty cents per bushel. He might easily get a thousand dollars for his corn crop. That would mean that he could clear all debts and buy another team of horses and more machinery. He might even rent still more land next year, for David would be big enough to run a cultivator.

Yes, things were prospering. He had not seen Hilda since that night when they had talked so long together, but he would see her soon and really find out about the land.

Then came a Sunday when the Grimsens had one of their company dinners. There were six different Danish families with all their children. It was a long hard day for Meta, especially in her condition, for it would not be more than two months until she would be delivered. The women all helped her in the kitchen that day. Most of the time they would not even let her stand by the stove, but made her sit in a chair and each one took turns visiting with her.

On these occasions there was always much friendly gossip and laughter over the peculiarities and limitations of those who were not present. The funniest story that day had been about Mrs. Snellson who always put her children's diapers to soak in her churn. She was reported to have said that it takes less water to soak them there and since it was a glazed clay churn Satan himself couldn't filthy it.

But there was other talk that day. Meta soon sensed that something was wrong. That people were talking. One said, "Now isn't it too bad you are to have another baby, Meta?" Another asked if it was true that Peter had already rented the widow's land again for next year. Thus the words buzzed. Peter Nielsen said openly at the table in a broad joking manner, "Now that Peter is a sly one. Does anyone here know how much rent he is paying on the eighty? Is it share or cash, Peter?" And Peter had said rather curtly, "Cash." Then the oldest man in the company, who had been many years in this country, said, "Don't ever buy a hat till you have tried it on."

Before the day was over Meta could see how the wind was blowing. It did not surprise her. Ever since that night when Peter had not come home till midnight, she had known there would be talk. She trusted Peter, but she also feared him. He was so dark in spirit at times. She did not believe what some people seemed to think, but she feared for the future. She knew that there was too little scope in her house for him, and that this ever bearing children made it as difficult for Peter sometimes as it was for her. If this one could only be a girl she would never have another.

As the days passed and she knew that Peter had again visited the widow, and had not even told her about his visit, she grew more and more fearful. What if he should leave her? Then what would happen? She knew how he often suffered because his sons were almost strangers to him. They never sought his company nor talked with him at night except to answer his questions, about either their work or their school. Alfred often left of an evening without asking permission. Peter was almost afraid of him, because he seemed to realize that if he rebuked him, he might throw the words back in his father's face.

Night after night as the winter came on the boys would go to their nickel novels upstairs and leave Peter brooding by the fire. One night Meta said openly, "Now, boys, you better stay down and talk to your father a little." They acted nervous and ill at ease as though they didn't know what to say, and then he spoke up. "Let them go, Meta. They would rather read their books upstairs than talk to their father. Nice sons I've got. A stranger would be more welcome to them than I am." With these words he got up, put on his hat and coat, and walked out. She heard his steps crackle in the snow as he went by the side of the house that led to the road.

"Now see what you have done, you awful kids,"

said Meta. She sat down by the table and began to cry. This aroused wonder and consternation, because the boys had seldom seen their mother cry, and not over anything that seemed so trivial to them as this did. To them this was just another stormy outburst of the kind they had seen so often.

"But, mother," said David, "what did we do?"

She didn't answer, but continued sobbing until they were thoroughly frightened.

"Where do you think Dad is?" said David.

"I can tell you where he is," said Alfred, "he is. . . ."

"Now, Alfred, you keep quiet," said his mother through her tears, and then without warning, she said, "Alfred, carry Karl up-stairs. The rest of you go up there too. Then, Alfred, I want you to come back and hitch up the team and go for Mrs. Kirkman."

She no longer cried. While Alfred went without a word to the bedroom and got Karl and carried him up-stairs, she went to the kitchen stove and put on two large kettles of water. When Alfred came down again she was packing the stove full of cobs.

Alfred put on his coat and hat. "Shall I stop on the way and tell Dad?"

"No, son. Just be careful in your driving for I shall need Mrs. Kirkman before morning."

When Alfred had gone out, she sat for a time by the stove looking very old and tired. She bent over in her chair and her face twitched with pain. Every ten minutes she had to put more cobs in the fire.

When a half-hour had passed and she tried to stoop

to the cob box again she suffered such acute pain that she cried out—almost screamed. "Now, I can do no more," she said out loud, and going to the stairway she called David. He came running so fast he almost fell down the stairs.

"David, tomorrow morning you will once more have a little sister to make up for the one who died. I must go to bed now. Will you stay up and keep the stove hot so that this water can boil?"

"Yes, Mother, but are you very sick?" he said in a scared tone.

She took his head in her hands and kissed him on the forehead. "No, not very, and you don't need to worry. I shall be well again before the next sun rises."

Alfred came with the midwife at twelve o'clock. An hour later Meta gave birth to a son.

It was three o'clock that night before Peter Grimsen came home. His face was pale and haggard as he stood by the stove and warmed his hands thoroughly. He barely said "How-do-you" to Mrs. Kirkman, and to Alfred and David who were still up he did not say a word. When he had turned himself many times by the stove until all the chill was gone from his clothes and he knew that his tremble was an inward chill which could do no harm in the bedroom he walked with a slow quiet step to the door and entered.

Meta was quiet and her eyes were closed. He laid his hand on her hot forehead. After a little she spoke in a barely audible tone, "It is another son, Peter."

After a long pause he bent over her and said, "You have had more to bear than is right. I have been a bad man to you." Quietly but more strongly than before came her answer, "No, Peter, that I will not listen to from anyone."

8

It would soon be Christmas now. Meta was in the kitchen again. She seemed very pale and was always too tired to do her work as it should be done. Peter had ordered David to get up first in the mornings to build the fires and make the morning coffee. After two weeks had passed David usually found his mother in the kitchen before him. She said it was a shame that he should come down in such cold weather to start the fires.

Peter was much kinder to the boys than ever before. He was quieter and sadder too. Whatever his thoughts were about that night when the last baby was born, he kept them to himself. Meta never spoke of the widow or the land. Peter noticed that when he talked of more land, she did not answer him. She seemed to have lost all interest in the farm.

Then one day a letter came that bore the inscription of a law firm in Weeping Willow. It was very brief. Alfred read it aloud to his father.

Dear Mr. Grimsen:

You are hereby notified that your lease expires by March 1st, 1906. It will not be renewed. You are asked to vacate by that date.

Yours truly,
JOHN CULVERT, *Atty.*

So it had come at last as Meta always said it would. Peter Grimsen had given seven years of his life to building up a rent farm and now he was ordered to move. What he had done to stop erosion by damming up ditches, changing the layout of the fields, and seeding permanent pasture had been partially to his advantage. That was the ordinary procedure of the thorough farmer in his class. He could not expect the landlord to make him concessions on that score. There were other improvements for which he felt that he had deserved more recognition than the owner seemed inclined to give him.

The good crop he had just harvested had filled him with a new hope and courage. He had begun to feel that he belonged in America and that he belonged on this farm. There were times when he almost forgot that he was only a renter and as such had no rights not guaranteed in writing. And now the writing had come to an end. It was the greed and envy of Paulsen which had finally brought this about, but to know that as a fact was no consolation nor in itself offered a solution. It seemed to Peter Grimsen as though his foothold were slipping. All the new resolves he had made since that night when his last child was born vanished into thin air as he stared at the writing he could not read. He asked Alfred to read it to him again, and as his son read Peter tried to follow each word on the page.

Well, there could be no mistake. He would have to move. He went outside. Before his eyes stood the evidence of his labor. Hog houses, fences, corn-cribs, three of them, each with a thousand-bushel capacity, a chicken house, a cob house, and a cattle shed—these were the buildings he had put up on this farm in the seven years he had lived there. When he came there was a house and barn and a small chicken coop. That was all. The rest of the improvements, which now made his place look so impressive to him, he had built. Every stick of lumber that went into those buildings, he had paid for. Those buildings were part of his life blood. His children had gone bare-footed in summer and without proper clothing in winter to pay for those buildings. They were his. He had paid a sharper price for them than anyone could know. But on the table in the kitchen lay a little letter that told him to move off. That was very easy to say, but where should he move? Should he rent another farm just to start this all over again?

He would go to see the landlord again. But that would be a waste of time. He knew that well enough. His previous trouble with this same landlord had made it clear that no appeal to his sense of justice would be of avail. More rent had settled it that time, but now it was no doubt not a question of rent. He guessed that Mr. Paulsen had bought the farm. Peter had also learned that the law forbade his removing anything that was made a permanent part of the farm. Thus he could not legally tear down the buildings he had erected, even if it would have paid him to do that for the sake of having the lumber to use on a new farm, should he rent another.

Defeat had come again. After the fierce battle with nature's forces had given him a partial victory and a new hope, a little piece of paper which represented what was known as law and order blew all of his hope away as easily as a summer breeze blows the down of a moulting goose.

Peter did not know much of the language of this new world, but he knew the difference between right and wrong. That was what he thought as he stood looking over his buildings. He believed that there was a right which could exist in spite of the law, but his belief was of small worth when put to the test. He was to learn more as time went on about that too. There were still many things to be learned in America that he had not dreamed of in Denmark.

This new problem cast its shadow over their Christmas. Meta tried to give the home a little of the spirit of happiness, but she was still too weak from her confinement to do much for the children. Peter was moody again, but different too. He scarcely ever spoke crossly to the boys. One day in early January he said to David and Hans in Meta's presence, "I want you boys to go down to Mrs. Schneidermann and tell her that we have to move from this place. Tell her that I cannot rent her land again next year."

Meta saw how hard this was for Peter to say, and she was sorry for him. After the boys had left, she said, "Peter, this has been a hard year for you. Let us try to forget it. Let us forget it all and go back to Denmark."

Peter was startled. It was as if her words had stirred

a deep and fearful thing in him. For seven years he had buried those words in his own heart. It was as though an old, almost forgotten tragedy were again to come back with its full force to make him suffer.

"What is it you are saying, Meta? Is it Denmark?"

"Yes, Denmark," said Meta almost fiercely. "Denmark is where we should be. Every year has grown worse instead of better. We have lost our daughter. I will never have a daughter now. America has taken that from me. We are insulted and abused at every turn. My heart aches for the children growing up without good schooling and always left out from parties and and ordinary social life. Why do you suppose Alfred goes with those older men to card parties and goodness only knows what other evil? It is because he has never had friends of his own age. I can't stand it any longer. Peter, can't we go back now? If we have a sale our stock and machinery and everything will bring quite a lot. We won't come home empty-handed."

"No. We would probably come back to Denmark with a thousand kroner. That would be one-fourth of what we had when we left there ten years ago."

This was but the beginning of many discussions. Meta held to her resolution that they should give up and go home. It was quite clear to Peter, as well, that Denmark was still home, but whenever he thought of leaving America his heart sank. Every day he walked out over the fields, even through the snow at times, and each walk seemed to increase the longing to stay.

He now saw for the first time the pathetic and

poverty-stricken character of their house. Outside the house there had been development and expansion. His many buildings indicated that, but in the house itself things were much as they had been when they first came there. One room, the parlor, had been success- fully papered, two years after that first failure, but the kitchen and the upstairs were even worse. More plaster had fallen from the wall, so that now there were great patches on ceilings and the bare lath showed. He realized that Meta had many times hinted at replaster- ing, but these suggestions had always been answered by a long enumeration of debts. There was no question of debts, however, when it came to building a new hog house or buying a new plow.

Peter could not make up his mind. The end of January came and still he was in doubt. A year ago it might have been easy for him to sell out. At that time Denmark possessed its old appeal for him. It was not the same now. He longed to visit Mrs. Schneidermann and discuss it with her. There were times when he walked in her direction, but he always turned back. That night when the baby was born had shown him how limited a man's life could be. His deep sense of duty and his loyalty to Meta and the children must not be sacrificed. There were plans that stole into his mind at times, catching him unawares, but as soon as Peter, the Danish farmer, husband, and father, saw them, he cast them out of mind. At such times he would decide to sell out immediately.

Then one of the first days in February he went to see

Mr. Van Doren. He went there in the morning. They talked till noon, and he stayed for the dinner, but not until he had asked Mr. Van Doren to send one of his boys to tell Meta where he was and that he would stay for the afternoon. The afternoon passed and he stayed for supper.

It was nine o'clock when he came home. Meta seemed almost jolly when he came into the kitchen. She had understood the meaning of that message. It had been like a long letter of confession to her, for it was the first time in the eighteen years of their married life that Peter had ever troubled to do a thing like that.

Hans was the only boy still up, and he was astonished and very embarrassed when he saw Peter come straight up to Meta and kiss her. He had never seen his father do that before. Badly as he had wanted to hear what his father had to say about the Van Dorens, he now said good night and hurried upstairs.

"Did you have a good visit, Peter?"

"Yes. The Van Dorens are fine people. They said I must bring you over some day. Couldn't we have a cup of coffee? The Americans can't make coffee, that much is certain."

"Yes. I'll put it on this minute."

As they sat over their coffee Peter told of many things he had discussed with Mr. Van Doren, but he found it very difficult to come around to the thing that had kept him so long at his friend's home that day. Meta knew that he was holding something back. Finally she said, "Did you tell Mr. Van Doren that we were planning on selling out and returning to Denmark?"

"Yes, I did. But he wouldn't listen to it. That's really what we talked about all day. He knows of a farm for rent that is much better than this one. It is a half section and is only two and a half miles from Weeping Willow. It's northwest of town. He says it's good land and that it has a better barn than this place and fairly good outbuildings of every kind." Peter didn't say anything about the house, because he wanted Meta to ask him. He had learned many things in the last month. Had he talked this farm over with Mr. Van Doren before Christmas he would not even have asked about the house. After he had heard about the barns and hog houses he would have been satisfied. But today the first question he asked was about the house. And now Meta asked the question.

"Oh, the house," said Peter, as though he had forgotten. "Yes, both Mr. Van Doren and his wife say it is a fairly good house. It is two stories and in good repair. You see the landlord himself has lived on the place. He is still living there, but plans to rent it out now and retire to town, so you can be sure it is in good condition. Now, what I wonder is shouldn't I go to see it, because there is really no hurry about going back to Denmark. We can always do that. My mother used to say, 'measure your cloth ten times, you can only cut it once.' "

"By all means go to see the place, Peter, for I am afraid we must stay in America, not next year only but always." There was a mingling of both sadness and joy in her voice, as she continued, "Alfred came to me today and said that if we went to Denmark, he wouldn't go along."

"He did," said Peter. "He said he wouldn't go along?"

"Yes, that's what he said. Can you see how it would be, Peter?"

"If he stayed here, his brothers would come over here to him one after another as they grew up, and we would sit alone in our old age. America is our home now for good or ill. Today I discovered that for myself, and I don't know but that I am glad."

Peter was much moved. Not since the day they had first decided to come to America, had he been so deeply stirred by a decision. Neither one of them had thought that the children would object to leaving, but now they saw clearly that already this land was their home and that Denmark would be a foreign country to them. A brief ten years had bound them to this land. Silently day by day the road back for Peter and Meta had been torn up, the bridges burned, and the guide signs destroyed. While they had been facing east in their dreams their thoughts and actions had been turned west, until now they were a part of the new world.

"Alfred and David are going to take turns helping me learn to speak better English," said Meta.

"That's good," said Peter, and then as if to show that he also was going to do something, he said, "Mr. Van Doren is going to help me take out citizenship papers."

This story is an attempt to give an imaginative picture of a past that seems farther away in time than it is in reality. No situation or character is meant to be a copy of actual people or definite situations. There is not to my knowledge in Nebraska a town named Weeping Willow.